DREAM IT.
PIN IT.
LIVE IT.

DREAM IT.
PIN IT.
LIVE IT.

MAKE VISION BOARDS WORK FOR YOU

TERRI SAVELLE FOY

Terri Savelle Foy Ministries
PO Box 1959
Rockwall, TX 75087
www.terri.com

Published in association with The Fedd Agency, Inc., a literary agency.

ISBN13 Hardcover: 978-1-943217-07-6
eISBN 13: 978-1-943217-08-3
ISBN 13 International Tradepaper Edition: 978-1-6803-1472-4

Cover and Interior Design by: Lauren Hall

Printed in the United States of America

First Edition 15 14 13 10 09 / 10 9 8 7 6 5 4 3 2 1

CONTENTS

INTRODUCTION...........................IV
Why You Need a Vision Board

CHAPTER ONE...............................I
Give Yourself Permission to Dream:
What Do You Have the Audacity to Imagine?

CHAPTER TWO............................23
The Power of the Pen: Clarity is Key

CHAPTER THREE..........................33
Setting Your Top Ten Goals: The 30-Day Challenge
that Can Change Your Life

CHAPTER FOUR..........................45
Design Your Board: What Goes on the Board?

CHAPTER FIVE............................55
Display Your Destiny: Why Is It Important to See It?

CHAPTER SIX.............................65
Once the Board is Up: Change What You're
Saying and You'll Change What Your Seeing

CHAPTER SEVEN................................79
The Law of Attraction in Action: What Are You Currently Attracting?

CHAPTER EIGHT................................99
Don't Share Big Dreams with Small Minds: Who Should See Your Dreams?

CHAPTER NINE................................III
What to Do While You're Waiting: Successful People Have Successful Habits

CHAPTER TEN................................135
The Hidden Key to Living Your Dreams: What Gets God's Attention

CHAPTER ELEVEN................................149
Ideas to Get Your Creativity Flowing: Places to Go, Things to See, Aspirations to Achieve

CHAPTER TWELVE................................157
Vision Board Success Stories: Be Inspired by Others Who Dared to Dream

APPENDIX A................................169
Host a Vision Board Group or Party

APPENDIX B................................177
Vision Board Samples: A Variety of Dreams Displayed

INTRODUCTION
Why You Need a Vision Board

> YOU WILL NEVER LEAVE WHERE YOU ARE
> UNTIL YOU SEE WHERE YOU'D RATHER BE!
> —UNKNOWN

If you've read very many success books or immersed yourself in the world of "personal development" then you have surely heard about the importance of having a vision board in order to get what you wish for!

The world became aware of the significance of vision boards with the launch of *The Secret*—a DVD unmasking the hidden reality of "the law of attraction." With success coaches worldwide sharing personal experience with their own vision boards, as well as Oprah Winfrey urging viewers to design their dreams, many people have unleashed their crafting skills by "framing their future."

In 1993, a nine-year-old girl was asked by her teacher to make a vision board. She pinned a photo of the singer, Selena (known as the Queen of Tejano music at the time) holding her Grammy award. That little girl grew up to become an international pop star—one of the bestselling artists of all time—and is on the Forbes list of "Top-Earning Women In Music." That little girl was Katy Perry.[1]

In high school, DeAndre Cortez Way made a list of all the things he wanted to achieve in his journal. The list included: (1) get a record deal, (2) have a

> YOU WILL NEVER LEAVE WHERE YOU ARE UNTIL YOU SEE WHERE YOU'D RATHER BE!
> —UNKNOWN

number one song, (3) have a platinum album, (4) invent a dance everyone would do. One year later, he checked everything off his list. DeAndre Cortez Way, better known as Soulja Boy, is an American rapper, record producer, actor, and entrepreneur who was listed at Number 18 on the Forbes list of Hip-Hop Cash Kings of 2010.[2]

Surrounding yourself with images of your vision causes your dream to become more alive inside you. It is a vital component of your success that you surround yourself with what "can be" and not just "what is." That's the power of vision.

A vision board adds clarity to your dreams and desires by allowing you to see them. It helps you concentrate and focus on your specific life goals. Basically, it keeps your attention on your intentions.

I decorated my bedroom wall. Right next to my bed there was this big wall that I decorated all with pictures. I hung up pictures of strong men, bodybuilders, wrestlers, and boxers and so on . . . I was DRIVEN to think big and to dream big. Everyone else thought that I was crazy![3] What you do is create a vision of who you want to be, and then live into that picture as if it were already true.[4]

—Arnold Schwarzenegger on the process of achieving his bodybuilding dream of becoming Mr. Universe.

Vision boards and vision board parties have become popular over time, but the majority of those using them do not realize that God is the one who wants us to be clear on our vision.

"Where there is no vision, the people perish."
– Proverbs 29:18 [KJV]

Let's break that scripture down into more plain language: perish means die! The Bible says very clearly that we will die without vision. Vision keeps you alive. It takes you from where you currently are to where you long to be! All the way back in Genesis, God told Abraham, "Go outside and look up at the stars, for as many stars as you can see, that's how many descendants you are going to have." (See Genesis 15:5) He later told Abraham to look at the grains of sand because it also represented his number of future descendants. He wanted Abraham to have a picture of it in his mind—to be able to visualize it.

Consider this: Abraham lived in the desert. What was he surrounded by all night long? Stars. What was he surrounded by all day long? Sand. God knew it wasn't enough for Abraham to hear about his future; he also needed to see where he was headed. He was literally surrounded by vision. Consequently, he became what he beheld.

When you create your vision in the form of a vision board, a vision book, or even an app on your smart phone, you are seeing yourself the way you want to be. I have been using vision boards for years, and they have kept me in a continual state of progression.

Having a vision board will help you on many levels, including:

- prioritizing your goals,
- obtaining clarity in your life purpose,
- building your faith in God's ability to perform the impossible,
- boosting your confidence and self-esteem, and
- reminding you of your mission.

When you're surrounded by ongoing negative messages that life will never get any better, your vision board will serve as a visual reminder of where you are headed. It will keep you focused when you are tempted to give up. It keeps you single-minded and full of faith.

What Is a Vision Board?

A vision board is simply a collage of pictures and images depicting your dreams. What you post can range from places you want to go and things you want to have to aspirations you want to achieve and your deepest desires in fulfilling your personal life goals. It is portions of your life assignment displayed in a way that you can keep them in front of you daily as a reminder of what you are dreaming for.

Why Does a Vision Board Work?

It's not that the board itself causes your dreams to magically appear; it's what the realization and clarity of your dreams does for you that makes it "work"! Personally, I have experienced the fulfillment of a wide range of dreams (and simple desires) in my life through the ongoing practice of having my vision clearly before my eyes. I've realized dreams such as:

- new dishes for my kitchen,
- my daughter's school tuition,
- conceiving a baby,
- purchasing a house,
- driving my dream car (debt-free),
- paying off debts,
- vacationing in dream locations,
- publishing my books (and seeing them in book-stores nationwide),
- hosting events in convention centers,
- speaking at some of the largest success conferences in the US,
- publishing my books in French,
- seeing my books for sale (in bookstores) in Paris, France, and
- even something as simple as owning a designer handbag!

By having my eyes focused on a clear, compelling vision for these dreams, they were achieved. God even said, "All that your eyes can see is yours . . . ." So, isn't it time you fix your eyes on your future?

If you see nothing, I am convinced you can expect nothing. If your life hasn't progressed over the past five years, then perhaps you need vision—and a clear one at that. Just as you 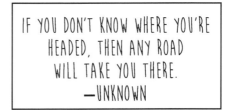 would never get in a car and drive having no idea where you're going, you shouldn't live your life without a clear, mapped out destination in mind.

IF YOU DON'T KNOW WHERE YOU'RE HEADED, THEN ANY ROAD WILL TAKE YOU THERE.
—UNKNOWN

This book will, most likely, push you out of your comfort

zone. That's good. Complacency is the greatest enemy of possibility. You will be challenged to open your imagination and have that childlike faith to believe that anything is possible.

What's in front of you is far more important than what's behind you. God wants you so focused on where you're going that you won't even consider looking back at where you've been. Of course, you learn from your past. Yes, you turn your messes into a message for others, but you should never spend time reliving, rehearsing, and remembering the past when God has so much for you to accomplish in your future.

Paul said in Philippians, "This one thing I do, forgetting those things which are behind, and reaching for those things which are before, I press toward the mark for the prize of the high calling in Christ Jesus" (Philipians 3:13 KJV).

Reach for those things which are ahead! In order to reach for them, you have to be clear on what "those things" are. Your dreams and goals need to be clarified. That's where your personal vision board comes into play. So, before you start cutting and pasting away, let's put a demand on your faith to dream bigger and get clear on what you need to pursue!

YOU'VE GOT TO CREATE DREAM BOARDS. YOU'VE GOT TO PUT THE NEW CAR UP ON YOUR MIRROR. PUT THE WEIGHT YOU WANT TO BE UP ON THE REFRIGERATOR. IF YOU CAN SEE IT IN YOUR MIND, YOU CAN HOLD IT IN YOUR HAND.
—STEVE HARVEY

ONE
GIVE YOURSELF PERMISSION TO DREAM
What Do You Have the Audacity to Imagine?

THERE ARE THREE TYPES OF PEOPLE IN THIS WORLD: THOSE WHO MAKE THINGS HAPPEN, THOSE WHO WATCH THINGS HAPPEN, AND THOSE WHO WONDER WHAT HAPPENED.
—MARY KAY ASH

As you begin to dream, you are going to have people tell you you're being foolish or that you're living in a fantasy world. You may even tell yourself that; but, daring to dream, having the audacity to imagine more for yourself is the only way to move beyond where you are right now.

A little boy in the sixth grade named Steve who came from a low-income family, wearing hand-me-down clothing and suffering from a stuttering problem, was sitting in class listening to his teacher as she gave them a new assignment. She asked the class to write down what they wanted to be when they grew up.

Steve had seen a man on television who was very funny and that became his dream. He decided he wanted to be on television making people laugh. The teacher began calling out students' names and sharing with the class what they had written down. When she came to Steve's paper she stopped. "Little Stevey, come up to the front of the class."

Proudly, Steve walked to the front of the class thinking she was going to encourage him and cheer him on!

"Stevey," she said, "Why did you write that on your paper?"

Steve answered, "Because I want to be on TV."

She said, "Who do you know on TV? Anybody in this school ever been on TV?"

"No ma'am," answered Steve.

"Has anyone in your family *ever* been on TV?" she asked.

"No ma'am," Steve said.

The teacher told him to take his paper home and write down something more realistic.

Steve was confused. Up until that moment, nobody had ever told him what he could or could not become.

That very night, Steve shared with his father what happened at school. Showing him the paper where he wrote his dream, his father advised him to read his paper every morning before school, every night before bed and thank God that one day he will be on TV!

Year after year, he did that. Today, Steve Harvey is on television every day making people laugh.[5]

Destiny Decisions

Someone once described the game of football as 60,000 people who desperately need exercise watching twenty-two men who desperately need rest. The game of football parallels life itself. The average person watches from the sidelines and very few ever really get off the bleachers to get in the game! Isn't it time you started playing in the game of life?

Recently, I saw a car commercial describing two different types of people on the road: drivers and passengers. Passengers are simply along for the ride. They sit back, look out the window, and let others decide on the direction they are going. Drivers are in control of their destination. When they make a wrong turn, they take responsibility and get back on the road. They know where they are headed. By the time you finish this book, you will no longer be "along for the ride." You will be strategically steering your life in the direction you choose to go. And you will arrive at your desired destination.

We all come to a fork along this road where we must make destiny decisions. One of the greatest realizations you will ever come to is when you realize that there is only one person responsible for the outcome of your life, and it's you. You, and you alone, must take one hundred percent responsibility for where you are, what you have achieved, your health, your wealth, your debt, your body, your success, your relationships, your current reality.

Zig Ziglar said, "Many years ago as a young, aspiring speaker, I heard an older speaker who was quite philosophical say that you are where you are because that's exactly where you want to be." Ziglar confessed, "I was broke, in debt and down in the dumps . . . It came through loud and clear that I was where I was and what I was because of the decisions and choices I had made in my life."[6]

Your decisions affect your destiny! Are you going to just go with the flow of traffic or go the narrow road that leads to success? Remember this: only dead fish go with the flow.

Motivational speaker Jim Rohn taught how there are certain emotions that can actually lead to an overall life change. One of those emotions is the feeling of disgust! Typically, we don't equate the word disgust with positive action; however, becoming disgusted with your current circumstances can actually serve as vision and momentum to get you out! For example:

- Seeing a photo of yourself overweight can be enough disgust for you to say, "I've had it! I have a vision to get in shape!"
- Having to put your groceries back because you lack the funds to afford them can be enough disgust for you to say, "Enough is enough! I have vision to increase my income!"
- Another breakdown in your car during rush hour traffic can be enough disgust for you to say, "That's it. I have a vision for a new car!"
- Maintaining the same salary for the past ten years can be enough disgust for you to say, "No more! I have a vision for promotion!"
- Your credit card declined at the restaurant in front of your friends can be enough disgust for you to say, "I'm making a change now! I have a vision to be debt-free!"

Disgust is what you feel when you're tired of being embarrassed, ashamed, and humiliated with where you are, and you develop a compelling vision to change!

It all starts with making a decision to take 100% responsibility for where you are today and where you're headed tomorrow. And that's exactly what you are doing right now or you wouldn't be reading a book about vision.

In Dr. Dave Martin's book, *The Twelve Traits of the Greats*, he tells the story of a man named Tim who reached that emotion of utter disgust with himself. Tim grew up in a middle class family of five brothers and one sister. At the age of eleven, he lost his dad in a tragic car accident. Tim struggled all through school and into college. Because of the pent up anger he had inside due to his father's death, Tim began using drugs. He felt sorry for himself; he was mad at the world, and destruction was the result.

Eventually, his decisions resulted in a prison sentence when he was caught selling drugs. In that cold prison cell trapped behind bars, Tim had a defining moment. He began to realize that he had no one to blame but himself. He woke up. He took full responsibility for where he had landed in life.

He began investing in himself by reading books constantly. As his mind began to expand, so did his dreams. He began organizing prison talent shows where he was the emcee. A naturally gifted comedian, he began to embrace his talent for humor.

Once released from the penitentiary, he was able to land a great job at a talent agency. Not long after, people began to notice him. Tim even turned down a role from Disney to play a major role in a TV show. He had his own vision for his life, and he began to pursue it wholeheartedly.

His dream was to star in his own TV show that reflected his personality and sense of humor. It was a show about a handyman on TV, and that show became a major hit called *Home Improvement* starring Tim Allen.

Thirteen years after his release from prison, Tim Allen was starring in the top TV program in America, had the #1 book on the *New York Times* bestseller list and had the lead in major motion picture, *The Santa Clause*.[7]

It all began when Tim Allen reached a level of disgust with where he was and began making a *destiny decision* to change! He obtained a compelling vision of where he wanted to be in life and began taking steps to achieve it. He went from a drug-pusher to a box office millionaire!

Don't Settle Where You Are

In Genesis 11:31, we read the story of Abraham and his father, Terah, who left the city of Ur and set out for Canaan (the Promised Land). Terah fully intended to lead his family into this land of abundance; however, the Bible records that Terah "stopped along the way and settled in Haran."

He was essentially saying, "This is good enough. It's not what I wanted, but I can survive here." Many times, we do the same thing when we set out to achieve our dreams and goals. It doesn't happen as quickly as we wanted. It appears hopeless at times. We don't have the support of those around us. We end up settling for less.

Abraham's father missed out on an opportunity God had for him. He stopped short. He settled for much less than God had promised him because he stopped dreaming. Don't settle! God has so much more for you. Give yourself the permission to dream bigger.

I read a story Joel Osteen shared in his book, *Your Best Life Now*, about a famous mountain climbing resort in the Swiss Alps that caters to businesses. They encourage their employees to climb the mountain and build team spirit.

> YOU CANNOT BE WIMPY OUT THERE ON THE DREAM-SEEKING TRAIL. DARE TO BREAK THROUGH BARRIERS, TO FIND YOUR OWN PATH.
> —LES BROWN

They meet at the bottom of the mountain for a pep talk and can hardly wait to climb to the top and take their victory photo together. About half way up the mountain, there sits a beautiful Alpine restaurant with a breathtaking scenic view. About noon, the weary hikers trail into this restaurant, take off their hiking gear, sit by the fire, eat a delicious lunch, and enjoy a hot cup of coffee.

Interestingly, after they are well fed and comfortable, less than half continue the climb to the top. Less than half! The story revealed that this majority who decide to stay are not incapable of climbing to the top nor is the climb too difficult for them; it's simply that they have tasted a bit of success and decided that it's good enough. They are satisfied with what they have accomplished.[8]

What a shame it is to quit before you reach your goal! Never settle where you are. Never be satisfied with what you have when God has so much more for you! He never intended for you to reach a certain level and plateau. He desires for you to climb to new heights, explore new horizons, and dream as big as you possibly can.

Don't limit God. He is capable of doing impossible things in your life, but you can actually prevent Him from doing them by thinking small. If you think in terms of "just enough to get by" then that's exactly what you will produce in your life.

You Have the Audacity to Dream That?

What do successful people have in common? What does it take to go from wishing things would change to living your dreams? In one word, it is audacity! This is a powerful word that can alter the rest of your life if you will be brave enough to obtain it. Audacity is having nerve, courage, daring, boldness, fearlessness, grit, and the willingness to take risks.

In 1976, a young Austrian bodybuilder with a thick accent, a name nobody could pronounce, and a box office disappointment under his belt, audaciously declared to a sports columnist, "I'm going to be the number one box office star in all of Hollywood." Arnold Schwarzenegger had the audacity to dream.

Trying not to show doubt or shock over Arnold's big dream, the reporter asked, "How do you plan to become Hollywood's top star?"

"It's the same process I used in bodybuilding," Schwarzenegger explained. "What you do is create a vision of who you want to be and then live into that picture as if it were already true."[9]

When you develop the audacity to dream, to get out of the mundane or the rut you may have found yourself in, people will think you're crazy. They will laugh at your dreams. You must remember that they aren't dreaming the same dreams you are. Who cares if they laugh? This is your life, your future, your destiny that is on the line. Will you cower down to the opinions of others or will you develop the boldness to live big?!

You must have the audacity to believe that you can achieve your impossible dreams. The key word in that sentence is *you*. You will achieve in your life what you believe you can achieve.

Schwarzenegger reminds us of this powerful truth:

> Even though there are so many people around that would say, 'no,' you will never make it because you have an accent, your body is too big, and your name—Schwazen, Schnitzel, whatever, who can pronounce that? But you know! It doesn't matter if anyone knows and if anyone else believes it. All you have to do now is go towards that vision. If you have a

very clear VISION of where you want to go and if you're willing to put the work in no matter what it takes to get this vision to turn into reality, then [you] can accomplish basically anything you want.[10]

What do you have the audacity to dream? What do you have the nerve to believe you can achieve in your life? What do you have the courage to pursue? I want you to develop such grit in your life that people say to you, "You have the audacity to believe that can happen?" You confidently respond, "As a matter of fact, that's exactly what I have: audacity!"

Some people say that achieving success is like knowing the combination to a lock. If you know the combination, it doesn't matter if you're male or female, 16 or 65, have an IQ of 35 or 135, the lock has to open. Unfortunately, most people are going through life without the combination. I want to reveal to you the combination to living your dreams.

Your Life Is a Reflection of Your Thoughts

Before you ever achieve success, you must first have the audacity to believe in yourself and your dreams. Your beliefs are simply a reflection of the dominating thoughts being entertained in your mind. According to Proverbs 23:7, you become what you think about. That is the law of attraction summed up in one scripture verse.

During an appearance on the Oprah Show, Jim Carrey admitted to the audience that before he ever hit stardom or achieved success, he visualized himself succeeding. As a struggling young Canadian with no money he drove his old truck up Mulholland Drive in Los Angeles every night and would visualize having directors interested in him. He would imagine people he respected actually saying to him, "I like your work."

In 1985 or 1987, says Carrey, "I had nothing at that time. But it just made me feel better. I would drive home and think, 'I do have these things. They're out there. I just don't have a hold of them yet.'"[11]

The images you visualize in your mind become your reality. Your mind is like a magnet. Whatever gets in your mind and stays there, you will attract in your life. This law works positively and negatively. If your mind is constantly thinking negative thoughts, you will attract negative circumstances. If you're constantly thinking you are worthless, you will attract people in your life who treat you as worthless. If you're constantly thinking poverty thoughts, you will attract a poverty lifestyle.

At the same time, if your thoughts are positive, you will attract positive circumstances. If you're constantly expecting good things to happen for you, you will attract favorable opportunities. It really is that simple.

Literally, like attracts like. Your thoughts are the pathway to your destiny. Your life today is a reflection of the dominating thoughts you allowed to take up residence in your mind yesterday. That may be hard to swallow; but, according to Proverbs, it is the truth. Your life today is a result of your thoughts about yourself yesterday. The good news is: you can change your thoughts!

> A MAN BECOMES WHAT HE
> THINKS ABOUT MOST
> OF THE TIME.
> —RALPH WALDO EMERSON

"Whatever a man thinks in his heart, so is he."
— Proverbs 23:7

"Many of you have heard me share the story of growing up in rural Mississippi . . . at the time we were called colored people—negroes. And, my grandmother was a maid. That's all she ever knew. The only real expectation she ever held for me was that one day I would, one day, become a maid, and in her words, 'Have some good white folks' (meaning people who would not speak negatively about me, who would allow me to take food home, who would be good to me and treat me with some level of dignity and respect). That was my grand-mother's dream for me. But I had another dream for myself. I had more than a dream for myself; I had a belief for myself.

"I remember watching her hang out clothes on the line one day, and say to me, 'You have to watch me, Oprah Gail, because one day you'll have to do this for yourself.' And knowing inside myself that that was not going to be my life. I don't know how I knew it, other than that thing that we all have—intuition or an instinct—that said, no, this will not be my life. But, because I sensed that and was con-nected to that . . . I knew that I will not be hanging clothes on a line in a backyard in Mississippi . . . and that belief that that would not be my life is what I held onto for the longest of times. I just, no matter what, believed that there was something bigger, greater, more for me."[12]

—Oprah Winfrey

There were two blind men in the Bible who approached Jesus asking if He would restore their sight. I think it's interesting how Jesus put the responsibility back on them and simply asked one powerful question, "Do you believe I am able to do this?"

Their response says it all. I want you to notice that without hesitation, they replied, "Yes, Lord." Think about that. Without questioning, without discussing, without trying to figure out how this could happen, they just believed.

Then, the Lord said, in response to them, "It shall be done to you according to your faith." (See Matthew 9:29) *The Message* translation communicates this verse another way, "Become what you believe." When you get to a place in your life where you can imagine God asking you that same question, "Do you believe I can do this for you?" and you respond (without hesitation), "Yes, Lord!" then you are ready to achieve the impossible!

I believe God is saying to you today, "Become what you believe." If you can believe to live in that house, if you can believe to own that business, if you can believe to weigh that amount, if you can believe to be healed in your body, if you can believe for restoration of your family, if you can believe to pastor that church, you can become what you believe.

In 1969, my dad was the owner of "Jerry's Paint and Body Shop" in Shreveport, Louisiana. His business was failing and suffering from enormous debt, his marriage was falling apart, and he was running from God as fast as he could. One night out of desperation, he finally surrendered his life to God and cried out, "Lord, I'm a failure! I'm a nobody. What would you even want with my life?" On the inside, he heard these words, "Don't worry about it, son. I am a master at making champions out of nobodies."

That very moment, he started believing he was a

champion. He changed his thinking. He changed the poor self-image he had into that of someone who could achieve impossible dreams. Currently, he has seven offices in various locations around the world, an international television broadcast airing in over 200 nations, has written over 70 books, and made an impact on humanity. Bottom line, he had the audacity to believe that God could use a paint 'n body man to change the world!

To Dream the Impossible Dream

Think of yourself, imagine yourself, and see yourself living your dreams in your mind. Everything gets its start in your imagination first. You have to hold on to the thoughts that agree with your dreams. You become what you think about most, but you also attract what you think about the most.

My parents celebrated their honeymoon in 1966 at Six Flags Over Texas in Arlington, Texas. As they walked through the amusement park, hand-in-hand, they stopped at an outdoor pavilion featuring local talent singing and dancing on stage. One young man began to belt out a powerful song that soon became their theme for life; it was titled, "To Dream the Impossible Dream," and my parents have done exactly that and done it well.

God has given you two types of sight: natural sight and spiritual sight. Natural

> IF YOUR DREAMS SEEM POSSIBLE, YOU'RE NOT DREAMING BIG ENOUGH!

(or physical sight) sees what's all around you. Spiritual sight sees within, sees the invisible, and sees what others can't see. Some call it seeing with the "eyes of faith." The Bible reveals story after story of people like you and me who put a demand on their faith to see impossible dreams come to life:

- Abraham and Sarah waited years to conceive a baby (I can totally relate to that). She had to get an image of that impossibility on the inside of her before God could perform the miracle of Isaac.
- The lady with the issue of blood had to see herself touching the hem of Jesus' garment before she could achieve her dream of divine health.
- David had to see himself killing Goliath before he ever released the stone.

What do you need to see inside before God can produce it on the outside? Do you need to see yourself:

- rising to the top of the company?
- singing before thousands of people?
- paying off your credit card debt?
- graduating from college?
- pastoring a church?
- hosting your own TV show?
- selling your first house?
- weighing your ideal weight?
- vacationing in Honolulu, Hawaii?
- driving the car of your dreams?
- having a family?

God loves being able to show us how well He does the impossible, so dream big enough for Him to do that.

Visualize Success

The most successful people in the world visualize their

desired results in life. They are very clear about what they want to achieve. Unsuccessful people are hazy, unclear, and uncertain about tomorrow. They just wake up and see what happens.

God said in Isaiah 43:19 [NIV], "See, I am doing a new thing! . . . Do you not perceive it?" In other words, He is getting ready to pour His favor on you, promote you, increase you, expand your influence, but He's asking you the question, "Do you not perceive it?"

> IMAGINATION IS EVERYTHING.
> IT IS THE PREVIEW OF LIFE'S
> COMING ATTRACTIONS.
> —ALBERT EINSTEIN

To perceive means to notice, to identify, to comprehend, and to see. God is asking you today, "Do you see it?" Do you see where he wants to take you? In other words, are you preparing for more? Do you have a clear vision? Can you see beyond where you are today? Are you anticipating promotion? Can you imagine big things happening in your life? You cannot have a larger life with a restricted imagination.

Your imagination is extremely powerful. It is the birthplace for all great ideas and dream pursuits. If you can't imagine it, you'll never have it. I am so convinced of the mind's ability to conceive an idea (using your imagination) before you ever materialize it in your life that I wrote a book titled *Imagine Big*.

Your dreams should be impossible. They should stretch you, challenge you, and force you to grow.

Any successful person who has achieved admirable dreams has had to take a giant step of faith into the impossible! Walt Disney, for example, was known to be an impossibility thinker. He was constantly seeking to conquer things no one had even considered. In fact, it's been said that when he would meet with his Board of Directors, he would toss out ideas across the table. If everyone agreed on the idea, then he would tell them that was NOT what they were going to do.

Again, he would toss out ideas. If everyone told him it was impossible and that nobody had ever done that before, he would inform them that was exactly what they were going to do![13]

> MOST OF THE THINGS WORTH DOING IN THE WORLD HAD BEEN DECLARED IMPOSSIBLE BEFORE THEY WERE DONE.
> —LOUIS D. BRANDEIS

Walt Disney was an impossibility thinker. And you should be, too!

I have discovered that God wants your dreams so big and so outside the realm of possibility that there is no way your dream can occur unless you use your faith! Hebrews 11:6 tells us that it is impossible to please God without faith. I interpret that to mean: If your dreams are impossible, and you have no idea how this could ever happen unless God comes on the scene and helps you, then you've probably got the right dream.

In Hebrews 11:1 [NLT], it says, "Faith is the confidence that what we hope for will actually happen; it gives us assurance about things we cannot see."

> IF YOU'RE GOING TO THINK AND YOU'RE GOING TO DO SOMETHING, DO IT BIG.
> —DONALD TRUMP

God desires for you to have that kind of faith. He wants your total dependency on Him to see these dreams manifest. You are making God smile when you dream impossible dreams.

Let me remind you that God enjoys using ordinary people to do extraordinary things. He believes in you much more than you believe in yourself.

Everything begins with your ability to envision, imagine, and conceive that image inside. When you sit quietly with God, you should be able to see more than you see when your eyes are open. If it makes you breathe deep

> I AM ALWAYS DOING THAT WHICH I CANNOT DO, IN ORDER THAT I MAY LEARN HOW TO DO IT.
> —PABLO PICASSO

and think, "This is big!" Great! You're on the right track.

Warning: the number one question that will stop you from dreaming big is: "How?" Don't ask that question! It's not your job to figure out the *how*. Your job is to dream and dream big.

See Beyond Today

There's power in just taking time to see beyond where you are at today. Project forward five years into the future and imagine your ideal life. Do not give thought to what is possible or not possible. Just get a clear picture of what you desire to have. When you think in terms of what would give you the greatest peace in your life, what do you imagine? What would you be doing?

- Are you married?
- Do you have a baby?
- Are your kids in college?
- Are you working?
- Where do you work?
- Are you self-employed?
- Are you ministering?
- Are you teaching a class?

- Did you write your first book?
- Did you go on your first mission trip?
- Are you living overseas?
- Is your debt paid off?
- What are you driving?
- Is your car paid for?
- How much money have you saved?
- Where have you traveled?
- Where do you live?
- What does your house look like?
- Are you at your ideal body weight?
- Who are you helping?

What does your life look like five years from now?

> THE TRAGEDY OF LIFE DOES NOT LIE IN NOT REACHING YOUR GOALS, THE TRAGEDY LIES IN NOT HAVING ANY GOALS TO REACH. IT ISN'T A CALAMITY TO DIE WITH DREAMS UNFULFILLED, BUT IT IS A CALAMITY NOT TO DREAM.
> —DR. BENJAMIN MAYS

Think about what comes to your mind when you read the following statements:

- What would you want to accomplish before you die if you were told you had one year left to live?
- What have you always wanted to do but haven't done yet?
- How do you want to be remembered?
- What is God speaking to your heart to accomplish?
- What activities do you want to experience?

- How would you spend your last twenty-four hours?
- What would you do if money was not a problem?
- How would you live your life if you didn't have to work anymore?

Thinking about where you want to be in the future helps you decide how to live today! Decide where you want to end up in life. Plan your life down to the last detail and then let God go beyond that. Do not be worried, anxious, or concerned about the process of getting from where you are to where you want to be. Just dream, imagine, and focus on designing your ideal life.

God has so much more for you than what you presently have. Your greatest days are ahead of you, not behind you. You must enlarge your vision, see what's ahead for you, and get motivated to fulfill your unique life assignment down to the last detail. In order to do this, you must have the audacity to dream!

Why am I so passionate about seeing you fulfill your vision, dreams, and goals? Because we don't have time to waste! I don't want you to repeat this year what you did last year. Now is the time for you to get clear on what God wants you to do with your life and start taking action.

You Have a Mission Here on Earth

Some people say that life is like a carousel—sometimes you're up, sometimes you're down, sometimes you just go round and round. Some say that life is like a deck of cards, you just have to play the hand you're dealt. Others claim that life is a journey, a dance, a battle. Personally, I believe life is an assignment. God has given you a unique assignment to complete during your time here on earth, and then it's over. You either turn in the assignment complete or incomplete.

This is the scripture that drives me: "I glorified you on earth by completing down to the last detail what you assigned me to do." (John 17:4 MSG)

It's time to aim for your future, full speed ahead, and it all begins by giving yourself permission to dream . . . and to dream big!

When Did You Last Give Yourself Permission to Dream?

I received this email from Lilly in Florida:

> I guess it was when I was in my 20s, that I stopped allowing myself to dream. Convinced myself that dreams are just fairy-tales, they are silly and hurtful for girls like me. I felt I needed to deal with the reality and the cruelty of life. Terri did awaken something that was buried deep in my heart, something wonderful, never to be hidden again.
>
> Today, here I am 65 years old, writing in a book of dreams all those things that I believe will bring some joy into this dull heart. I can see it all. I am having fun doing it and it's not silly at all. I even set myself some goals and started working at making it happen. You are never too old.

It is so important not to waste any time, but that doesn't mean you should give up or feel you've failed because you aren't where you thought you'd be at your age. What Lilly said is true. You're never too old to start working toward a dream.

Proof that Your Age Does Not Matter

Age 18 months – Brooke Shields lands her first commercial as the Ivory Snow baby.

Age 8 – Mozart composes his first symphony.

Age 12 – Jesus astounds a group of religious leaders with his wisdom and insights.

Age 18 – Mick Jagger debuts with his new rock band, the Rollin' Stones. (The band will add the "g" eventually.)

Age 21 – Steve Jobs introduces the Apple computer, created with young colleague Steve Wozniak.

Age 31 – Bill Gates makes his first billion dollars.

Age 40 – Lucille Ball debuts as Lucy Ricardo in the TV comedy *I Love Lucy*.

Age 44 – Sam Walton founds Wal-Mart.

Age 53 – Walt Disney opens a theme park in Anaheim, California called Disneyland.

Age 58 – Frank Sinatra, retired for two years, reignites his career.

Age 65 – Winston Churchill takes office as Britain's Prime Minister.

Age 69 – After 22 years of work, Noah Webster publishes the landmark *An American Dictionary of the English Language*.

Age 70 – George Brunstad becomes the oldest person to swim the English Channel.

Age 71 – After 27 years in prison, South African Nelson Mandela gains his freedom.

Age 77 – Astronaut John Glenn returns to space on the space shuttle Discovery mission.

Age 78 – Grandma Moses begins her career as a serious painter.

Age 79 – Ben Franklin invents bifocal eyeglasses.

Age 80 – Jessica Tandy wins her first Oscar for her role in *Driving Miss Daisy*.

Age 89 – Frank Lloyd Wright completes the Guggenheim Museum.

Age 90 – Swimmer Walt Pfeiffer sets six World Masters records at a meet in Long Beach, CA.

Age 100 – British actress Gwen Ffrangcon-Davies appears in the Sherlock Holmes movie *The Master Blackmailer*.[15]

> YOU ARE NEVER TOO OLD TO SET ANOTHER
> GOAL OR TO DREAM A NEW DREAM.
> —C.S LEWIS

ACTION STEP

Set aside ten minutes every day for the next seven days to sit quietly with no distractions to simply think and imagine your future.

TWO
THE POWER OF THE PEN
Clarity is Key

AND THE LORD ANSWERED ME AND SAID, WRITE THE VISION
AND ENGRAVE IT SO PLAINLY UPON TABLETS THAT
EVERYONE WHO PASSES MAY [BE ABLE TO] READ
[IT EASILY AND QUICKLY] AS HE HASTENS BY.
—HABAKKUK 2:2 [AMP]

In 1990, struggling actor Jim Carrey took his visualizing exercise a step further by writing himself a check for ten million dollars for "Acting Services Rendered." He gave himself five years to achieve his dream by dating it "Thanksgiving 1995." He carried it in his wallet, and it deteriorated over time. Just before November 1995, he found out he was scheduled to film *Dumb and Dumber* and for "acting services rendered" he was offered payment of ten million dollars![16]

Every day, Sara Blakely wrote down what she wanted to be: (1) self-employed, (2) invent a product that she could sell to a lot of people, (3) create a business that would be able to fund itself. Today, Sarah Blakely, the creator of Spanks, is a multi-millionaire who has appeared on the cover of *Forbes* magazine.[17]

In each story, these individuals had the courage to write down their dreams. This is one of the most vital, but overlooked, keys to success! And it's really not that hard! Your life can advance dramatically just by taking the time to grab a pen and some paper and begin to write what you want.

People who have dreams often do not see the importance of writing them down. As Scott Nicholson said in his book *Seeds of Achievement*, "Thinking you can keep your goals in your head is just an excuse for not writing them down." Something powerful happens when you put pen to paper.

One of the most fascinating studies of writing your dreams was conducted by the 1979 Harvard MBA program. Graduate students were asked, "Do you have clear, written goals for your future?" A shocking 3% had written goals and plans. Of the 1,000 students, 13% had some goals but never wrote them down. An alarming 84% had no goals at all. Ten years later, the same graduating class was interviewed and discovered that the 3% who had written goals were earning, on average, twenty times as much as the 97% of the class combined![18]

Writing Your Dreams and Goals Is a Clear Key to Success!

Dr. Gail Matthews, psychology professor at Dominican University, conducted research on the topic of goal-setting using 267 participants and found that simply by writing down your goals you are 42% more likely to achieve them.[19] I couldn't agree more. I have discovered this to be true in my own life as I have written down my dreams. Here are a few I have seen become reality through the years:

- Speak at the largest church in France
- See my books on the shelves at Barnes & Noble bookstores
- Sign with a French Publisher
- Meet, and speak at an event with, John Maxwell
- Save $100,000
- Pay cash for my BMW
- Vacation on the French Riviera

Henriette Anne Klauser, PhD. details the power that comes from writing things down in her book *Write it Down and Make It Happen.* When you write something down, you are setting your aim and putting your future in motion. The actual act of writing your goals down makes them real and tangible.[20]

Before you design a vision board, you simply need to write. This is what forces you to clarify what you really want. Imagine going to the airport and trying to purchase a ticket to just "somewhere." That doesn't work. No, you choose a particular destination. Writing your dreams and goals is no different. You are charting your course and deciding where you want to go.

Writing your dreams and goals enables you to stay focused so you are more likely to avoid distractions. When other opportunities come your way, even good ones, you will maintain your focus if your goals are in writing.

Suze Orman, author of *New York Times* bestseller *The 9 Steps to Financial Freedom* had a job at Merrill Lynch in her early career days. Stricken with fear that she wouldn't be able to meet her sales quota for the company, she decided to put pen to paper and write her goals.

"I created what I wanted for myself first on paper. Every morning before I went to work, I would write over and over again: 'I am young, powerful, and successful, producing at least $10,000 a month.'" She claims that writing her goals replaced her fears of inadequacy with "endless possibility." And she has far surpassed that target![21]

One of the best ways to get started is simply to identify your desires. It's very important that you get clear on what you really want. But don't treat it like homework. This is the fun part! You get to dream as big as you want. In your prayer time, practice sitting quietly with God and journal your thoughts. Simply grab a pen and paper or use your iPad and begin writing down your dreams and desires.

Hall of Fame football coach, Lou Holtz, did this very exercise back in 1966. He was only twenty-eight years old when he lost his job, had no money in the bank, a wife who was eight months pregnant, and two other children to feed. His wife, Beth, bought him a copy of the bestselling book, *The Magic of Thinking Big* by David J. Schwartz.

This legendary book suggests that you should write all the things you want to accomplish in your life before you die. So, Lou sat at his kitchen table and let his imagination run wild. He wrote 107 things he wanted to do. The list included:

- have dinner at the White House,
- meet the Pope,
- appear as a guest on The Tonight Show,
- coach at Notre Dame,
- win a national championship,
- land a plane on an aircraft carrier.

After reading that book and making his list, he realized

that by writing down goals that really mattered, he found ways to achieve them. But it all begins by writing, and writing as big as you can. So far, Lou Holtz has achieved 102 of the 107 things he wrote.[22]

> DON'T BE A SPECTATOR; DON'T LET LIFE PASS YOU BY.
> — LOU HOLTZ

How do you discover your destiny? As Joel Osteen puts it, "It's not complicated. Your destiny has to do with what excites you. What are you passionate about? What do you really love doing? Your destiny will be a part of the dreams and desires that are in your heart—part of your very nature."

Osteen continues, "Because God made you, and because He is the one who put those desire within you in the first place, it shouldn't surprise you that your destiny will involve something that you enjoy."[23]

So, write. Write as big as you can. Write from your heart. Do not let your mind tell you that it's impossible. Just write whatever comes to you.

Clarity Produces Results

H.L. Hunt, the man whose life was the inspiration for the TV series *Dallas* and the character, J.R. Ewing, was a man who rose from a bankrupt cotton farmer in the 1930s to become a multi-billionaire. He was once asked during a TV interview if he could provide advice to those wanting to be

> I CAN TEACH ANYBODY HOW TO GET WHAT THEY WANT IN LIFE. THE PROBLEM IS I CAN'T FIND ANYBODY WHO CAN TELL ME WHAT THEY TRULY WANT.
> —MARK TWAIN

successful. He responded by saying that only two things were required: (1) You must decide *exactly* what it is you want to accomplish. (2) You must determine what price you'll have to pay to get it . . . and the resolve to pay that price![24]

Identify Your Desires

What do you want? When was the last time you even asked yourself that question?

- Do you want to be debt-free?
- Do you want to lose weight?
- Do you want to travel?
- Do you want to design clothing?
- Do you want to be a missionary?
- Do you want to go to graduate school?
- Do you want to adopt a child?
- Do you want to be an actor?
- Do you want to record music?
- Do you want to own a boat?

Clarity about your dreams is the single most important step to success! You will be amazed at what you can accomplish in life when you get clear on your dreams and goals. Napoleon Hill did a study on the major causes of failure. He concluded that failure was due to a lack of a well-defined purpose in life. Ninety-eight out of one hundred people he analyzed had no aim and suggested this was the major cause of their failure. He states, "There is no hope of success for the person who does not have a central purpose, or definite goal at which to aim."[25]

Is it just luck that my books are translated in the French language? No. I have been crystal clear on my goal of having all of my books translated in French. Why aren't they translated into German or Italian as well? I never have set a goal to have all of my books translated into those languages.

Without putting your dreams in writing, you will wander year after year without even realizing it. It's similar to

what happens when you're at the beach floating in the water. You just lie there letting the tide take you farther and farther away. Suddenly, you look up and realize how far you've drifted from the shore. It is the same in life. One day, you wake up and wonder, "What have I been doing all these years?"

A Quick Way to Get Started

Sometimes it's good to just start with a few desires of your heart. That's pretty simple. Where would you like to travel? What would you like to drive? What would you like to own? How much money would you like to save by December 31st? Where would you like to work? Which university would you like to attend? Who would you like to meet? What does your ideal physical body look like?

Just get started. You may begin with basic desires of material things you would like to acquire. For example, your list may start along these lines:

- I want to have a house on the lake.
- I want to have a speedboat.
- I want to own a brand new BMW.
- I want to have a Louis Vuitton purse.

- I want to earn $100,000 salary.

That's okay. Start writing whatever comes to your mind. As you begin to write whatever pops into your head, you are putting a demand on yourself to dream. Open your mind up to the unlimited possibilities that are ahead for you. You haven't seen your best days. Perhaps you haven't dreamed in so long that your "dream muscle" may be totally out of shape. You need to practice identifying your true desires by just writing something.

Act as if you are a child and are being asked, "What would you like for Christmas?" Most children are not concerned with *how* their parents will afford the gifts or *if* they are asking too big. They just dream.

Without regard for how you can have what you desire, just dream. Use your imagination. Imagine it is five years from now and you are living the life of your dreams. What does it look like? Where do you live? Where do you work? Where do you vacation? What do you do for fun? What do you drive? How much money can you give away to ministries and charitable organizations? Just dream.

The more you write, the more you will realize what you really want. What do you want to do? You may start by listing fun, adventurous things such as:

- visit Paris, France,
- skydive,
- snorkel,
- meet someone famous,
- go to a Broadway show,
- ride horses on the beach.

The more you write, the more you will discover your

true ambitions. It may include more specific, meaningful things such as:

- I want to go on a mission trip to South Africa.
- I want to give $10,000 to help rescue girls from human trafficking.
- I want to volunteer at a women's shelter.
- I want to get my master's degree in counseling.
- I want to own my own hair salon.
- I want to write a book on financial freedom.

Don't hold back. Write as big as you can.

Dreams Are Given to You by God

In addition to all the stuff you want, the places you want to see, the adventurous things you want to do, God wants to speak to you about His plan for your life. He cares about all these other things, too. In fact, He is the one who gives us the desires of our hearts. Don't ever think of your dreams and desires as insignificant.

The Bible says that God will give you the desires of your heart. The Latin word for desire means "from the father." How do you know when it's a dream from God? When you can't let go of it!

Your vision and your vision board will be unique to you. This is all about your life, your desires, and your assignment from God. Some people get so stuck on deciding what to put on the wall that they don't create a vision board at all. I never start clipping away at photographs in magazines until I first sit quietly with God and dream.

I am giving you a big challenge to write 101 things you want to do with the rest of your life. Don't think about the actual designing of the vision board yet. We will get to that later. First, you need to stretch yourself by thinking.

ACTION STEP

MAKE A LIST OF 101 THINGS YOU WANT TO DO

Why do you need to list 101 things? I want you to put a demand on yourself to dream. Just when you think you cannot possibly conjure up another "place to see" or "thing to do" in your lifetime, keep dreaming. Let your imagination run wild. Create that childlike excitement without regard for how it can be achieved. They don't all have to be huge, expensive or adrenaline-pumping things. Just give yourself a reason to get up and do something.

In Chapter 11, I have listed a variety of ideas to get your creativity flowing. Fill up your own list with places you want to go, things you want to experience, skills you want to acquire, subjects you want to study, people you want to meet, and museums you want to tour. Dream as big (or as small) as you possibly can.

THREE
SETTING YOUR TOP TEN GOALS
The 30-Day Challenge that Can Change Your Life

> GOALS ARE SIMPLY DREAMS WITH DEADLINES.
> —NAPOLEON HILL

Brian Tracy says one of his favorite exercises is to imagine it is December 31st this year, and as he looks back over the year, he enthusiastically claims, "This has been the most amazing year of my life!"

What would have to happen in order for you to say something that bold? What would have occurred in your personal life, your finances, your family, your business for you to make such a declaration? Whatever your response is, those are your goals.[26]

An alarming 97% of American adults are trying to live their lives without clear, specific, written goals. Motivational speaker and author, Jim Rohn said that learning to set goals is a habit that altered his life forever!

Rohn recalls in *7 Strategies for Wealth and Happiness* how his mentor, Earl Shoaf, said to him, "Let's take a look at your list of goals so that we can review and discuss them. Maybe that's the best way I can help you right now."

Jim replied, "But I don't have a list with me."

Mr. Shoaf said, "If you don't have a list of your goals, I can guess your bank balance within a few hundred dollars."

Which he did!

That got Jim's attention! Jim said, "You mean that if I had a list of my goals my bank balance would change?"

Mr. Shoaf confidently declared, "Drastically."[27]

Goals Determine What Drives You!

Most likely, the importance of setting goals is not a particularly new concept for you; however, what's easy to do also is easy *not* to do. Brian Tracy, an entrepreneur, professional speaker, and expert on the subject of goal-setting, was working laboring jobs for years, living paycheck to paycheck, missing meals, sleeping on the floor of a little apartment when he came across a book that said, "If you want to be successful, you have to set goals. And you need to write them down."

"I sat down and made a list of ten things I wanted to accomplish in the foreseeable future," said Tracy. "Thirty days later, my whole life had changed! Almost every goal on my list had already been achieved or partially achieved!"[28] Today, he has taught over five million people in sixty countries how to become lifelong goal-setters.

Darren was eighteen years old, waiting tables and was invited to a seminar on the subject of goal setting. Before he turned nineteen, he was earning a six-figure income, then went on to become an entrepreneur and multi-millionaire and never looked back. Today, Darren Hardy is the editor of *Success* magazine and offers this advice in regards to setting goals, "I attribute it to the #1 skill that has given me more success than anything."

Darren adds, "I get to interview extraordinary people. The consistency I find among all these great achievers is this: (1) they are all committed to continual learning, and (2) they all have clearly, defined goals and a plan to achieve them."[29]

There probably isn't a person reading this book who hasn't heard the importance of having goals in writing; however,

> IF YOU'RE BORED WITH LIFE—IF YOU DON'T GET UP EVERY MORNING WITH A BURNING DESIRE TO DO THINGS— YOU DON'T HAVE ENOUGH GOALS.
> —LOU HOLTZ

if you walk up to the average person and ask to see their written list of goals, they don't have one!

In fact, that's exactly what Professor David Kohl from Virginia Tech did. In his research, he "discovered that 80% of Americans don't have any goals. Sixteen percent have goals, but don't write them down. Three percent have goals, they write them down, but don't review them." Only one percent, all in fact, millionaires, had goals, wrote them down, and reviewed them on a consistent basis. You cannot reach your full potential without goals.[30]

When we don't set goals, it's as if we are leaving our lives up to chance and are just waiting to see what happens. With goals, you can literally succeed on purpose.

Brian Tracy calls it "The Ten Times Factor." He boldly states, "You will achieve your goals ten times faster and with greater probability if you're absolutely crystal clear on what you want and how to get there."[31]

God wants you to have goals and intermediate objectives that you strive toward each year. It's one thing to have a big dream, but it's vital that you have smaller dreams (goals) that you can focus on now. Philippians 3:13-14 (KJV) says,

"This one thing I do: forgetting those things which are behind and reaching for those things which are ahead, I press toward the mark for the prize of the high calling in Christ Jesus." That "mark" refers to your goals.

According to statistics, 93% of New Year's goals go unfulfilled. In fact, 30% are broken within the first week! Among those who join a gym, 80% dropout within eight weeks![32]

Setting goals for your life means deciding what you want in life, planning how to get it, and then going after it! I am thrilled to say that I have learned how to make it into the 7% category of those who stick with their New Year's goals until they are achieved! I want you to get serious about achieving your life goals.

Mistakes in Goal-Setting

People get excited about goals, but they tend to set unrealistic goals in the beginning.

- I'm going to become a millionaire.
- I'm going to lose 50 lbs.
- I'm going to write four books.
- I'm going to drive a brand new Porsche.
- I'm going to save $500,000.

If you set goals that are too unrealistic, or may take longer than 12-18 months to achieve, it destroys your confidence and diminishes your hopes of achieving your dreams. Most success coaches recommend you set goals that have about a 50% chance of possibility. Set goals that stretch you, push you, and build your confidence.

The most common goals people set look something like this:

- Lose weight

- Save money
- Get out of debt
- Quit smoking
- Eat healthier
- Get closer to God
- Spend more time with family
- Read more
- Get house organized

Although these goals are common, they are a set up for failure. They are broad, unclear, and too vague to ensure commitment to their achievement. How do you go after all these random but important goals? With a clear, simple plan.

I have learned more about goal setting from Brian Tracy than anyone else. Years ago through his teaching, he introduced me to my "new best friend" (a.k.a., a spiral notebook) in order for me to take on the "30-Day Challenge" of writing out my goals.

Here is the "30-Day Challenge" I want to introduce to you:

1. Write your Top Ten Goals for this year (or the next 12-18 months).
2. For the next thirty days, write your ten goals once a day.
3. Write them in the present tense.
4. Write them down each day without looking back to what you wrote the day before. If you can't remember all ten original goals, that's okay. It just means that not all of them were that important to you. Stay focused on the ones that capture your imagination and motivate you to achieve.

5. Use a notebook.

In the following chapters, I will teach you how adding images to your goals increases your desire to achieve them. But for now, just start writing. If you will adhere to this exercise, you can achieve more in the next five months than you most likely have in the past five years!

In the previous chapter, I challenged you to think big, dream big, and imagine big. In this chapter, I want you to know that you can write as small as you want. What do I mean by this? One of the greatest ways to build your faith is to see results in smaller areas of goal achievement. You may want to have new dishes for the kitchen, so write it down. You may want to have dental work done, so write down the cost. If you want a new vacuum cleaner, research the cost and write it down. No goal is too small. The point is that it builds your confidence to continue setting higher goals.

Keep in mind, we always want to be sure our goals are in line with God's will for us. Consult the Lord and seek His guidance, submitting your will to His will. I once heard Joyce Meyer say at a conference, "I would rather ask God for everything and get 50% than ask for nothing and get 100%!" Meyer adds, "If God doesn't want you to have it, He won't give it to you anyway." Just inquire of the Lord, ask Him for what you want, and be sensitive to His leading.

Goal-Setting S.M.A.R.T. Tips

First of all, I really don't recommend setting more than ten goals. If you set five goals, that's great. If you set too many goals, you are likely to lose focus and not achieve any of them.

You've probably heard of the S.M.A.R.T. goals technique. The description varies from teacher to teacher, but here is my explanation to help you set and achieve your goals:

Specific: You must bring clarity to what you want to accomplish by being as specific as possible.

Wrong Example: I will save more money this year.
Right Example: I will save $5,000 by December 31st.

Measurable: This is where you can truly measure whether or not you hit a goal.

Wrong example: I will lose weight.
Right example: I will weigh 120 pounds by May 15th (current weight: 130 lbs.).

Action-Oriented: Use action verbs when setting goals, such as: reduce, save, earn, exercise, invest, enroll, run, etc.

Wrong example: I will be more consistent with exercise.
Right example: I will exercise five days a week.

Realistic: If your goals are too big, you are setting yourself up to fail. I encourage you to set goals that stretch you and cause you to grow but are also somewhat attainable.

Wrong example: I will save $50,000 by May 31st (from my salary of $70,000).
Right example: I will save 10% of my current salary = $7,000.

Timeline: Deadlines are motivating. Always establish a "by when" date. It keeps you motivated to achieve it. The most productive day of the year is the day before vacation. Why?

There's a deadline. The quickest way to clean your house is to invite company over. Why? There's a deadline.

Wrong example: I will write my book.
Right example: I will finish my manuscript by September 30th.

Set a STRETCH Goal

Challenge yourself to set at least one goal that you would consider your "highest expectation" and set your "mountain-moving faith" to achieve it. It could include finishing your book, singing before an audience, developing your website, publishing an article, completing your degree, get your pilot's license, pay off a lingering debt, obtain your realtor's license.

In order to be effective, we have to be stretched. Stretch yourself in the area you feel is vitally important to you this year.

My Personal Goals

The first time I practiced this "30-Day Challenge" of writing my goals down every day was in 2012. I wrote down my "highest expectations" for the year with no idea of how they would be achieved. My list included:

- Save $25,000 for Kassidi's car.
- Save $5,000 for our vacation to the Bahamas.
- Speak at the largest church in France.
- Receive invitations to speak in two new cities in France.
- Sign a new contract with my book publisher.
- Weigh my perfect weight of 110 pounds.

- Write a new book *Breaking Soul Ties*.
- Publish *Breaking Soul Ties* in French.
- Write a new book *Imagine Big*.
- Speak at the Amway Summit as the keynote speaker.

For thirty days, I wrote down this list of ten goals. When thirty days passed, I continued to review them by reading them out loud every day. I would set the alarm on my phone to go off at 10:00 each morning with a reminder that read "Goals." I expressed gratitude for each goal as if it were already attained. By December 31, 2012, every single goal was achieved! Since then, I have been setting and achieving goals consistently.

Focus is the number one key ingredient to achieving your big dreams and goals. You will get what you focus on (good or bad). You must

> WHERE THERE ARE NO GOALS, NEITHER WILL THERE BE SIGNIFICANT ACCOMPLISHMENTS; THERE WILL ONLY BE EXISTENCE.
> —ANONYMOUS

get laser-focused on what you want to achieve in the next twelve months. As we've discussed, what you think about, you bring about. For example, think about the color blue. For ten seconds, look at everything in the room that's blue. Then close your eyes and think about those items. Ready, set, go . . . 10-9-8-7-6-5-4-3-2-1.

Now, how many red things did you see? Nothing. Why? You weren't focused on red. You only saw what you were prepared to focus on—blue. It is the same way with your goals. When you focus on this list of goals, you will recognize opportunities all around you to achieve these dreams. You only recognize what you focus on.

It's no different than when you purchase a new car and

suddenly you see your type of car all over the road where you never saw it before. Your type of car was there all along, it's just now you are focused on it, so you recognize it. This principle applies to your goals. The more you focus on them by daily reviewing them, the more you will recognize opportunities all around you to achieve them. Opportunities were there all along; you just never noticed them until now!

You always get more of what you focus on. That's why it is so important that you focus on what you *do* want and not what you *don't* want. This "law of attraction" is about seeing what you're looking for. If you really don't know what you're looking for, you surely won't get it.

Every one of us have what is called an "R.A.S. filter" (Reticular Activating System). This filter is used to sift through all the sensory inputs we are exposed to all day. We would probably go a little crazy if we weren't able to weed out some of the stimuli coming at us on any given day. This R.A.S. filter is most easily explained this way: if you are in a room full of a few hundred people talking, and someone says your name through a crowd of noise, you hear it. That's your R.A.S. filter sifting through the noise to focus on something you're looking for.

When you get clear about your goals, you give instruction to your R.A.S. filter to start looking for the ideas, opportunities, resources, and relationships that line up with your personal goals. You start recognizing these things that are being attracted to you.

I used the illustration earlier of how you spot your car all over the road where you never noticed it before. Well, your new car is now at the forefront of your mind, and your R.A.S. filter has sifted through the other cars to cause you to recognize yours.[33]

The biggest key to success in any area is consistency. As

you are regularly writing down your goals for thirty days, you're consciously thinking about them every single day. This key behavior of repetition is what causes your desires to elevate and your motivation to skyrocket. You will get so determined to check off this list that nothing will stop you!

> SETTING GOALS IS THE FIRST STEP IN TURNING THE INVISIBLE INTO THE VISIBLE.
> —TONY ROBBINS

Years ago, Napoleon Hill was hired by Andrew Carnegie to do thorough research on the most successful people in the world. The result of this research was the classic book, *Think and Grow Rich*. His search involved interviewing 500 millionaires, including the most famous people of their day, such as: Thomas Edison, Henry Ford, Theodore Roosevelt, John D. Rockefeller, Alexander Graham Bell, John Wannamaker, Charles Schwab, etc. From this extensive research over twenty years, he concluded that each of these super-achievers had one thing in common: clearly, defined, written goals!

ACTION STEP
Take the "10/30 Goals Challenge"

You may (or may not) want to look over your extensive list created in Chapter 2 to pull ideas from. If you choose to sift through this list, narrow it down to what you feel is most important at this time in your life. It can include financial goals, family goals, physical goals, career goals. They can be as big or as small as you want as long as you feel that it has at least a 50% chance of happening.

- Use a notebook.
- Write your Top Ten Goals for this year (or the next

12-18 months).
- For the next thirty days, write your ten goals once a day.
- Write them in the present tense.
- Write it down each day without looking back to what you wrote yesterday.

Review the S.M.A.R.T. goals technique as you're listing them. Imagine it is December 31st, and you joyfully exclaim, "This has been the most amazing year of my life!" Think of what needs to happen in order for you to say that. Write down those goals.

> GOALS ARE NOT ONLY
> ABSOLUTELY NECESSARY TO
> MOTIVATE US. THEY ARE
> ESSENTIAL TO REALLY
> KEEP US ALIVE.
> —ROBERT H. SCHULLER

FOUR
DESIGN YOUR BOARD
What Goes on the Board?

Designing your Vision Board is going to be a fun exercise, but it is way more than a craft project. It is the expression of your dreams and goals in a tangible form so you have them in front of you for motivation and accountability. John Assaraf tells the story of what his boards did for him on his road to success.

He created a vision board of things he wanted to achieve. Whether he wanted to build a bigger business, acquire more money, or change his physique, he found pictures that represented what he thought those dreams would look like. While he was living in Indiana, he looked at his vision board every single day and visualized himself having acquired all the things he wanted to contribute on a daily basis.

"I moved three times from Indiana to L.A. to San Diego. I bought this house, renovated it and had all the furniture and all the boxes (that I moved away from five years earlier) brought to this house where I live right now. One morning, my son had come to my office, and he sat on these boxes that had some of my vision boards and goal boards inside.

"He asked, 'Daddy, what's in the box?'

"I said, 'Well, sweetheart, they are my vision boards.'

"At five years old, he said, 'What's a vision board?'

"I explained to him that a vision board is where I put my goals. He didn't understand. So, I pulled out a vision board (and you've got to remember these boxes had been sealed for five years). The first board had a wonderful little sports car that I bought, the watch that I bought and a couple of other materialistic things. When I pulled the second vision board out of the box, it had a picture of the house that I had bought a year earlier, and I didn't even know that I was living in it!

"I had bought my dream home that I had cut out of a dream home magazine five years earlier! Now that may seem amazing to you, but can you imagine how I felt! I started to cry because I finally had an understanding of what I was doing to my brain all those years ago."[34]

> IT HELPED ME BUILD MY COMPANY TO THE LEVEL THAT I WAS EARNING MILLIONS OF DOLLARS A YEAR. IT CAUSES YOU TO THINK IN WAYS THAT ARE MORE IN LINE WITH YOUR GOALS VERSUS WHAT YOU CURRENTLY HAVE.
> —JOHN ASSARAF

Frame Your Future

We are taught to frame our past by displaying photographs of what we've previously done and accomplished. But the opposite is true of your vision board. You are literally framing your future before it ever happens! This is the fun part!

Designing a vision board is one of the most valuable things you will ever do to see the realization of your dreams right before your eyes! If you've already taken the time to write your dreams and identify your top goals, now it's time to illustrate them visually.

Your vision board is a collage of images and symbols— visual representations of your personal dreams and goals. This is an incredibly useful tool to keep you motivated to achieve them. As you watch your dreams come to fruition one by one, you will be inspired to continue dreaming.

Most people think in pictures and images, not in words. When you think about the car you desire, you don't see in big letters, C-A-R. You actually see a photo of your car in your mind. Since your mind responds strongly to visual stimulation (your goals and dreams in pictures), it is important that you see your dreams before you.

Be creative and enjoy searching for images that are a tangible representation of where you want your life to go. Use current photographs, search through your favorite magazines, and search the internet for what you're looking for specifically. It can include pictures of things you would like to have one day but cannot necessarily afford right now such as: an exotic vacation, a luxury car, a new house, an expensive ring. It can also include photos depicting improvement in areas of life: greater health, a happy marriage, more children, or professional accomplishments.

Look for items that inspire you. Print or cut out all the images that represent your big dreams. It could be a photo of the headline reading "*New York Times* bestseller" or "Top Sales Winner" or "Grammy Winner." It could be a photograph of your dream sports car, your vacation home in Maui, or your chic apartment in Paris. That's fine. Go back to the chapter where you began giving yourself permission to see beyond where you are today.

Your S.M.A.R.T. Goals in Pictures

While I do believe you need to see where you are headed in the future by pinning your big aspirations, you also need to see your smaller, obtainable goals on this board as well. As soon as you start achieving these more attainable goals, it will motivate you to stay focused on the larger dreams for your life.

Referring back to your list of top ten goals for the year, go through each goal, one by one, and research images that illustrate each goal.

For illustration purposes, let's say a portion of your "Top Ten Goals" on your board could include:

Goal #1: Save $5,000.
Print out a photo of cash. Then, write the vision and make it plain. Clearly type or write across this photo (or near it): "Save $5,000 by December 31st."

Goal #2: Vacation in the Bahamas.
Place a postcard or a printout of the Bahamas, the resort you desire to stay at, or the excursions you plan to take. Research the cost to achieve this goal (include flights, hotels, meals, excursions, spending money, etc). Write the vision and make it plain: "Vacation in the Bahamas by July 31: $7,000."

Goal #3: Purchase new dining room furniture.
Research the furniture you desire. You can browse online, look through magazines, or visit local furniture stores and take a photo of you sitting at the dining table you desire.

Place the photos on your vision board as if it already belongs to you. Research the cost. Write the vision and make it plain. "Purchase new dining room furniture by Thanksgiving Day: $3,300."

Goal #4: Pay off my car.
You could take a "victory photo" of you standing by your car with your hands up celebrating your debt-free car! Call the bank and find out the balance remaining. Write the vision and make it plain: "I am driving a debt-free car: $7,436.08 by September 30th."

I recommend you keep it as neat as possible. When we get too many items on the board, it can create a snapshot of confusion. Be selective. Arrange your photos and your goals in an order that appeals to you. Too many items on the board can make it difficult for you to stay focused on the attainment of anything.

Personally, I prefer to have giant numbers next to each of my ten goals for the year. I have the number and the goal with a photo to match the goal. You can experiment with different designs and find the one that feels the best for you. You can choose colored or patterned backgrounds. You can use one or several photos for each goal. But, be careful not to spend too much time searching for the "perfect image" of your goal. It could cause you to become frustrated, lose momentum, and never put anything up.

Personally, I have one vision board at my house for my personal and family goals. I have an additional vision board at the office for my career and ministry goals.

Special Occasion and Theme Boards

Some people have several vision boards that represent specific themes or special occasions. For example, if you have a dream to take a cruise to Venice, you could design an Italian-themed board. Be creative and arrange photos of the sights you desire to see—the romantic gondola rides, St. Paul's Cathedral, the picturesque countryside, the delicious gelato, etc. Again, research the cost to afford this dream destination and write it down.

If your dream is to attend a specific college, you may want to design a university-themed board to include photos of the campus, sports events, a specific college degree printed out with your name written across it, images of a cap and gown signifying completion of your goal. Research tuition, room and board, and other fees necessary to achieve this goal. You may also want to put the word "scholarship" on this board, and start applying. After all, you have not because you ask not. Start asking.

If your vision is to build your dream home, you may want to design a house-themed board. It could include your desired floor plan, photos of interior design for specific rooms, spacious walk-in closets, desired furniture pieces, or lush landscaping photos. In addition to the images you desire, you should include financial goals attached to these dreams.

If your dream is to get married, you may consider a wedding-themed vision board. You could include photos of your ideal wedding gown or tuxedo. You can pin images of chapels, cathedrals, or dream locations for your fairy-tale wedding to your board. Wedding rings, floral arrangements, a wedding certificate—let your imagination run wild in depicting your heart's desire on this board.

Vision Board for a Family Vacation

I have one friend who had a "family vacation" vision board located at the entrance of her home. It was placed in a prominent place with frequent traffic on purpose. She wanted each of her family members to stay focused on the vision of going on a Florida vacation. Rather than just discuss the idea of going to a tropical destination one day, she had an array of exciting photos of the resort placed on the board. She wanted her children to see the beautiful palm trees, luxurious swimming pools, and exciting water parks. She also included photos of the many activities that this vacation would include such as attending the "happiest place on earth" (a.k.a. Disney World), roller coasters, Disney characters, along with photos of the ocean and the glistening sandy beaches nearby.

The enticing photos kept the family determined in the attainment of this dream vacation. The mother (and instigator of the vision board) wrote out the full amount for the family trip. She did the research on flights, hotel accommodations, dining, and tickets to the attractions. Underneath the vision board sat a small table with a box. The box had a little slit cut out at the top for donations or contributions to the goal.

Each time visitors and family members would stop by, they would inquire about the vision board (and the box) and want to contribute to this goal (myself included). When the children earned extra money or were given cash gifts for special occasions, it all went toward the vision. This middle class, single income family of eight went on their dream vacation to sunny Florida without going into debt!

That's the power of having a vision and a vision board consistently before your eyes.

Anyone can tack a picture onto a corkboard of a sports car, a mansion, and a wad of cash, but that's too broad. You need to be very specific about your desires. If you desire to have money in your savings account, then print a photo of cash, but also write out exactly how much you want in your account.

You will need:

- *A board* – This can range from a poster board at your local pharmacy or super market to a cork board from any craft store or office mart. You can use a magnetic board if you desire. There are also very crafty, upscale boards available at different stores. I use a simple cork board and wrap it with a beautiful, large frame to dress it up and display it as a decorative piece.
- *Pictures (Magazines, postcards, brochures)* – You will enjoy researching images to match your big dreams and your top goals for the year. Be as creative as you want. You can look through magazines and cut out photos or go online and research the dream and print it out. You can use postcards, newspaper clippings, brochures, etc.
- *Pushpins or glue* – You can decide which works best for you. I use pushpins so I can remove goals once achieved, and it doesn't leave a messy finish.
- *Other* – You will also need scissors, pens, markers, or stencil letters to prepare your images and write your goals on them.

The fun thing about designing a vision board is that it

is as unique as you are. Make it your own process. Some "crafty types" make the most beautiful, embellished vision boards that could be sold at an art auction. Some people just tack seven photos on a poster board and they're done. It's okay.

If you're one of those really creative personalities, you can add fancy stickers, cropped paper, embellishments, glitter, etc. Display your personality on this board. At the same time, don't paste so much bling that it loses its motivation toward achievement because it's just pretty artwork.

In contrast to the artsy types, don't allow the pressure of making it "fabulous" stop you from ever doing it. It doesn't have to be perfect; it just needs to be done. Remember, most people do not even know what they want, much less take the time to visualize their dreams and keep them before their eyes. You are miles ahead simply by following through with this project. And the good news is, you can always change it up as you go along.

It's a good idea to update your vision board annually. As goals are achieved, you can place them in your vision book as an encouragement and reminder that dreams do come true. (*For information on purchasing a "Dreams and Goals" notebook to store your completed goals, visit Terri.com.)

Have fun designing your vision board. This is your future and you get to frame it.

ACTION STEP

Schedule a time and commit to make a vision board!

FIVE
DISPLAY YOUR DESTINY
Why Is It Important to See It?

> THE MIND HAS THE MIRACULOUS ABILITY TO
> FIGURE OUT WAYS OF ACHIEVING
> WHAT IT THINKS ABOUT MOST.
> —BILL CHANDLER

After you design your vision board, it is vitally important that you keep these images in front of you consistently. This is not something you start on January 1st and put away in a drawer or closet until December 31st to see if anything happened. Your mind always moves toward the dominating images you keep before your eyes. Key words: "that you keep before your eyes."

Vision for a Hotel

Coming out of the Great Depression, Conrad Hilton, the founder of the Hilton Hotels, suffered big losses in the crash of 1929. One day, he came across an article that captured his heart. It was titled, "The Most Famous Hotel in the World." It was the iconic Waldorf Astoria in New York City.[35]

In addition to its world-wide recognition as being the tallest and largest hotel in the world, *Weekend at The Waldorf* was the first major motion picture filmed entirely in a hotel and drew the world into its luxuriousness. The film starring Ginger Rogers grossed $4,366,000 and ranked number seven at the box office in 1945.[36]

As young Conrad viewed the breathtaking images of the legendary hotel, God dropped a dream in his heart to own that very building. Knowing the power of having a vision, writing it down, and keeping it before your eyes, Conrad tore the pages out of the magazine, wrote across the photo, "The Greatest Of Them All" and slid it under the glass top of his desk. Daily, his vision was before him.

Naturally speaking, it appeared impossible. There were no odds in his favor; however, with each year that passed, he continued to believe. When he visited New York City, he would make it a priority to walk around the property praying, believing, and dreaming to one day own that hotel.

With the old magazine clipping still placed under the glass-top desk, eighteen years later, on October 12, 1949, one of Conrad Hilton's lifelong ambitions materialized as he acquired control of the Waldorf Astoria Hotel.

You are Transformed into the Image Before Your Eyes

The more you look at the images of your ideal future, the more you desire them. The more you desire them, the more persistent you become in fulfilling them. Your vision board needs to be placed in a prominent place where you will view it consistently. The old adage is true: out of sight, out of mind.

Remember this isn't for the purpose of doing a fun, little craft project. This is your visual reminder of what you are expecting to accomplish. You may need to place your vision board in a private place so others aren't viewing it and expressing their negative comments about the likelihood of it ever happening. That's okay. Just make sure it is in a place that you will visit daily. It needs to be easily accessible to you and ever-present before your eyes, not necessarily any-one else's eyes.

You Become What You Behold

There is a powerful principle found in the Word of God that reveals we become what we behold. In order to behold something, it does not mean to glance at it every once in a while. It means a constant, immovable, and firm gaze; to look at consistently and constantly.

In 2 Corinthians 3:18 (NASB), Paul writes, "But we all, with unveiled face, beholding as in a mirror the glory of the Lord, are being transformed into the same image from glory to glory, just as from the Lord, the Spirit." Notice this scripture says that we are "transformed into the same image." We are transformed into the same image as what? That which you are beholding. What you constantly look at, you become. This is the Law of Vision.

Joshua 1:8 tells us to behold the Word of God (do not let the Word depart from your eyes; keep it in the midst of your heart). Why? Because what you behold, you become!

Your vision for your future needs to be meditated on day and night. That word meditate is defined as thinking deeply or focusing one's mind for a period, engaging in reflection. Reflecting something means mirroring back an image.

You could say the images you think on deeply, focus on,

and engage in are a reflection or are showing you who you really are! It can be compared to those old Polaroid cameras. You focus the camera on a subject, and an image is developed right before your eyes. The point is that whatever you focus on will eventually develop in your life.

Most success coaches recommend starting your day and ending your day reviewing your dreams. That is how you keep them constantly before your eyes.

This Was God's Idea

Before you think of this as mind science or some mystical concept that veers off of Christian principles, let me remind you that this practice originated with God. He is the One who introduced this application to us all the way back to the first book of the Bible.

In Genesis, we see the story of "Jacob and the cows." Jacob had a large family to support and felt he needed to have his own land and his own herds of cattle. He had served his Uncle Laban for fourteen years and was ready to have a place of his own.

Laban wasn't in favor of him leaving because he was quick to realize that the Lord had blessed him because of Jacob. He urged him to stay longer and asked what he could do to encourage him to change his mind—what kind of deal they could make.

Jacob thought about it for a moment and then basically said, "I will stay with you on one condition. I take all the speckled and spotted cattle and give you the rest."

In those days, animals with spots or speckles were considered not as good as solid-colored animals. In addition to their lower value, there were also fewer spotted cows on Laban's property. It appeared Laban was getting the deal of the century!

However, what Laban didn't realize was that God had given Jacob a plan. In Genesis 30 and 31, we learn of the specific strategy God gave to Jacob in a dream. In this dream, God instructed Jacob to take poplar, almond and chestnut trees, strip off part of the bark so that the white tree trunk and the bark were left looking "spotted" and "streaked." He was then instructed to lay the spotted branches or "rods" in the watering troughs where the solid-colored cows frequently drank water and were forced to keep their eyes on them.

Additionally, when the cows were mating and when they were giving birth, the branches were to be visibly placed right before their eyes. The result: the solid-colored cows reproduced speckled and spotted offspring!

There is no logical reason, but the fact remains that those solid-colored cows simply became what they beheld. And that principle is still working today. You will produce in your life the images you keep before your eyes.

If It Will Work for a Cow

What they constantly kept their eyes on was produced in their lives. Theologians believe that Jacob walked away with nearly seventy-five percent of the livestock because of this strategy: what they saw is what they produced.

You know what I say? If it will work for a cow, surely, it will work for us!

What would happen if you continually beheld the images of what you want produced in your life? Remember Proverbs 23:7 (NKJV) says, "For as he thinks in his heart, so is he." In other words, what you think about, you bring about!

Vision Board for Healing

What are you beholding? What are you looking at? You need to see images of how your life *can* look. Stop looking at reality and thinking this is as good as it gets. You have to *see* something before you can have something.

In speaking about her experience, Dodie Osteen has described how her body began drying up with cancer. When she looked in the mirror, she vividly saw a frail, deteriorating body. She knew she had to keep a vision of health in front of her if she were going to get victory over cancer.

She went through all the family photo albums and found pictures of when she was in perfect health and looking alive and full of energy. She place those pictures around the house. Why? She needed to see herself healed and alive! She surrounded herself with what "could be" not simply what "was."[37] That is vision. That is your faith in action to acquire what you desire. And as a result, she is alive and full of energy today completely healed of terminal cancer! You do not have to settle for life the way it is. Surround yourself with what "can be" in your life as well. Make it a point to keep it ever present before your eyes.

I challenge you to commit to viewing, not just glancing, at your vision board every single day. Visualize yourself as already attaining these dreams. See yourself enjoying what you're visualizing.

Since I was a little girl, I would see replicas of different airplanes sitting on my dad's desk at his office. I just figured he was still entertaining his inner-child by maintaining "toys" to play with. Little did I know that he knew the power of vision and consistently keeping the vision before his eyes. He has owned nine airplanes through his organization exactly like the models that sat on his desk. Is that a coincidence? I think not. Your life is constantly moving toward the dominating images in your mind. You will attract in your life the images you keep before your eyes. It's the Law of Attraction. So what are you keeping your eyes focused on?

Once you've designed your dream board, you obviously can't physically carry it around with you. That's why I created the "Dreams and Goals" app for your smart phone. We never leave home without our phones, do we? This is just another way for you to have your vision, your goals, and your future aspirations clearly before your eyes at any given time.

Because of my traveling schedule, I am unable to look at my vision board each day; however, with my dreams visually represented on my app, I never go a day without viewing them, praying over them, and looking out for their completion with much anticipation.

The Importance of Visualizing

What is visualization? It is simply the use of the imagination through pictures or mental imagery to create a vision of what we want in our lives. Your mind is activated by pictures.

Visualization has been used since the beginning of time, and you actually visualize quite often though you probably aren't aware that's what you are doing. When you're hungry, you visualize what you want to eat. When you plan a vacation, you visualize where you want to go. When you have a big event, you visualize what type of clothing you want to wear. Your mind thinks in images and visualization.

It is used often in sports to help athletes improve their performance. Whether it's basketball players visualizing themselves shooting free throws or golfers visualizing their golf swing, even swimmers, runners, gymnasts, and skiers practice visualization to achieve their goals.

I heard a story about the Australian sailing team that had never won the America's Cup. In 1983, the coach thought he would try this "visualization stuff." He had a cassette tape made that included a narration of the Australian team beating the American team. It had sound effects in the background. You could hear the wind blowing, the waves crashing, along with voices energetically expressing excitement over each buoy they rounded while beating the Americans. This twenty-minute voice-over description felt real. They could truly imagine beating the Americans and winning the Cup.

The coach instructed the team to listen to this description on tape every day, twice a day for three years! When race day finally approached, the moment arrived when they were up against the Americans. Because of their ongoing practice of visualization, the attitude of the Australians was a confident, "Not them again! How many times do we have to beat these guys?" They had developed an entirely new stance. Their mindset was bold, audacious, courageous, assured. Consequently, they came in and won the America's cup![38]

The saying goes, "What happens out there is a result of what happens in here." In simple terms, this means that your reality is a result of what is happening in your head. One study looked at brain patterns in weightlifters and found that the patterns activated when a weightlifter lifted hundreds of pounds were similarly activated when they only visualized or imagined lifting.[39]

Brain studies reveal that thoughts produce the same mental instructions as actions. When you perform or rehearse an event in your mind, it creates what scientists call a "neural pattern" that teaches your muscles to do exactly what you want them to do. That's why sports coaches claim that "sports are 90% mental and 10% physical."[40]

God even said, in reference to the ungodly men building the tower of Babel, "This is only the beginning of what they will do. Nothing they have imagined they can do will be impossible for them." (See Genesis 11:6) He is communicating with us how powerful our use of the imagination or visualization is. If you can visualize it, that's the first step in doing it.

> I NEVER HIT A SHOT, NOT EVEN IN PRACTICE, WITHOUT HAVING A VERY SHARP IN-FOCUS PICTURE OF IT IN MY HEAD.
> —JACK NICKLAUS

If it's driving a new car, then close your eyes and pretend you are watching the scene of a movie. See yourself walking up to your car, lifting the door handle, opening the driver's side door, and as you slide into the seat you can smell the rich leather upholstery. Before you start your car, adjust the rearview mirror, lift the visor, position your seat just right, and before you pull out, sit there and thank the Lord for giving you the desires of your heart. Can you see it? Can you smell it? Can you feel it? Can you believe it? Then, go ahead and start thanking the Lord now!

This is how you visualize each and every one of your dreams. Now, do this again and again and again. Become what you behold.

ACTION STEP

Schedule sometime over the next seven days to go somewhere and be alone with God. Go somewhere quiet and get alone with God. Close your eyes and see yourself attaining every dream God has put in your heart. Clearly see the outcome you desire. When I say "see the outcome," I literally mean to imagine every dream as clearly and with as much detail as you can. Which emotions are you feeling as you experience this dream? Who is with you? What are you wearing? What is your environment like? Act as if you are truly experiencing the fulfillment of this dream.

SIX
ONCE THE BOARD IS UP
Change What You're Saying and You'll Change What You're Seeing

FOR OUT OF THE OVERFLOW OF THE
HEART THE MOUTH SPEAKS.
—MATTHEW 12:34 [ESV]

Your vision board is now designed, your goals are clear, your dreams are imagined, now what? You need to remove all negative self-talk about your life and replace it with positive declarations affirming your future. Your words are a tool to be used to help you reach your goals.

Your words can create doubt and negativity or they can position your life for something magnificent. What are you saying about your life? Your finances? Your family? Your health? Your career? Your very own words shape your world.

You cannot talk defeat and expect victory. Your words have creative power. If your dreams appear absolutely impossible and there is no indication that things will ever change, do not use your words to describe your situation; use your words to change your situation.

When I wasn't doing anything in this town, I'd go up every night, sit on Mulholland Drive, look out at the city, stretch out my arms, and say, "Everybody wants to work with me. I'm a really good actor. I have all kinds of great movie offers."

I'd just repeat these things over and over, literally convincing myself that I had a couple of movies lined up. I'd drive down that hill, ready to take the world on, saying, "Movie offers are out there for me, I just don't hear them yet." It was like total affirmations.

-Jim Carrey, Actor[41]

One of the greatest things you can do to see the images on your vision board come to life is to speak them out of your mouth. It's time for you to learn what could be a "foreign language" to you. This is the language of God in which you no longer speak of the problem, you speak of the solution. Literally, you prophesy your future.

It is vitally important that you silence the negative "mind chatter" taking place from the moment you wake up until you go to bed. You know, that silently loud inner voice that limits you from achieving your dreams? We all battle with negative thoughts.

- Who do you think you are?
- How could that ever happen to you?
- You'll never live in a house like that!
- You'll never have that kind of salary!

When your negative thoughts are entertained in your mind long enough, they will eventually start coming out of your mouth. Matthew 12:34 (ESV) says, "For out of the overflow of the heart the mouth speaks." *The Message* translation of this verse says, "Words are powerful; take them seriously. Words can be your salvation. Words can also be your damnation."

Your words carry immeasurable significance. Your experiences in life are affected by the words you've spoken in the past. Your life tomorrow will be determined by the words you speak today. You have the ability to change the entire direction of your life with that little thing under your nose. It's as simple as it seems.

Successful people take a proactive approach to their dreams. They don't wait to see what happens with their lives. They prophesy their future. They speak an entirely different language. What is this language? They speak of their dreams before they manifest *as if* they already have them.

What most don't realize is that this powerful, life-altering application came straight from the Word of God. This entire world was created with words. (See Hebrews 11:3) God said, "Let there be..." and there was (the sun, the moon, the stars, everything). In fact, the Bible tells us that we serve a God who speaks of "nonexistent things" as if they already exist. (See Romans 4:17) He expects us to apply the same principle. That's what Jim Carrey was doing whether he knows it came from God's Word or not.

Unsuccessful people speak of things the way they are as if they will always be that way. And the truth is, as long as you continue to declare negative statements over your life, then that's exactly what you will continue to experience.

Have you caught yourself saying things such as:

- "Nothing good ever happens to me."

- "I'm drowning in debt!"
- "This marriage will never improve."
- "No matter what I try, I'm still fat!"
- "I'll never finish college!"
- "I could never afford a house like that."
- "I'll be the last one to get married!"
- "Losing weight is so hard!"
- "I never succeed at anything!"

We are literally trapped by the words of our mouths. How you frame your words will be how you frame your world. You cannot speak negative words and live a positive life. You could interpret this to mean, "Anything you say can and will be held against you."

> WHAT'S COMING OUT OF YOUR MOUTH HAS EVERYTHING TO DO WITH WHAT YOU ARE EXPERIENCING.

This may or may not be an entirely new revelation to you that your present condition is a product of your words. Determine today that you will not let one negative comment come out of your mouth about yourself and your circumstances again. You believe yourself more than anyone, so cut that stuff out of your vocabulary.

Your words have the ability to destroy and the power to build up. We read in Proverbs 18:21 (AMP), "Death and life are in the power of the tongue, and they who indulge in it shall eat the fruit of it [for death or life]." Every time you open your mouth to talk, you speak life or death.

Famous People Who Prophesied their Deaths

Sources indicate that one of the greatest American writers

that literature has ever known, Mark Twain, joked publicly that "the next time Halley's Comet passed close to Earth, he would go out with it." The

> IF YOU'LL CHANGE WHAT YOU'RE SAYING, YOU'LL CHANGE WHAT YOU'RE SEEING.
> —JOEL OSTEEN

last time the Comet had been visible was in 1835 (the same year Twain was born), and Halley's Comet passes us only once every seventy-six years. The Comet appeared on April 20, 1910, and Twain died the next day of a heart attack.

One of the fifty greatest NBA players of all time, "Pistol" Pete Maravich had been playing in the league for four years at the age of twenty-six years old. In an interview with the *Beaver County Times*, Maravich said, "I don't want to play ten years [in the NBA] and then die of a heart attack at the age of forty." Pete completed exactly ten years in the NBA (as predicted), and eight years later was playing a pickup game of basketball when suddenly, he collapsed and died of a heart attack at the young age of forty.

Rapper Tupac Shakur just two months before he was murdered in a drive-by shooting on the Las Vegas strip in 1996 spoke in a song of dying from a gunshot. In a PBS interview, Shakur was asked, "Where do you see your life over the next few years?" His response, "Best case, in a cemetery."[42]

Rapper Dolla sang in "Georgia Nights" about dying just months before he was shot at a PF Chang's restaurant in Los Angeles at only twenty-one years old.[43]

In Napoleon Hill's book, *Think and Grow Rich*, he shares the story of the power of words that is downright chilling:

In a Midwestern city, a man by the name of

Joseph Grant, a bank official, "borrowed" a large sum of the bank's money without the consent of the directors. He lost the money through gambling. One afternoon, the Bank Examiner came and began to check the accounts. Grant left the bank and took a room in a local hotel, and when they found him, three days later, he was lying in bed, wailing and moaning, repeating over and over these words, "My God! This will kill me! I cannot stand the disgrace!" In a short time he was dead. The doctors pronounced the case one of "mental suicide."[44]

Hopefully, you are not speaking death-related words over yourself or prophesying your funeral, but what other detrimental words are coming out of your mouth?

In the Bible, James 3:4 tells us that a rudder controls the entire direction of a ship the same way our tongues control the direction of our lives! God is pointing it out plain and clear to us that our words direct our lives, positively or negatively.

In other words, you may think your dreams will never come to pass, but don't speak it. You may think you're not qualified for the promotion, but don't speak it! You may think you'll never conceive a baby, but don't speak it. You may think that your debt will linger on for another ten years, but don't speak it. Why? Your words have power.

It's not okay to be critical with yourself. Start asking yourself, "Is what I'm about to say what I want to come about in my life?" If it does not line up with your dreams on that board, then don't voice it.

In the book of Luke, an angel appeared to Zechariah

and informed him that he was going to have a baby and instructed him to name the baby John. Overcome with doubt, Zechariah responded with unbelief, "Are you sure? Do you know how old I am?" Are you responding with the same negativity because of your current age?

Let's see how the angel responded to those negative words. He said, "Because you doubted, you will remain silent and not speak until the baby is born." He literally zipped his lips! The angel knew that if he allowed Zechariah to "speak his mind," he could forfeit the whole plan of God for his life. Think about that. For nine solid months he could not speak. That's how detrimental our words can be over our future. (See Luke 1:18-20)

Another powerful illustration is found in the book of Jeremiah. God gave Jeremiah a promise that he would become a prophet to the nations. Immediately, Jeremiah began to respond with words of inadequacy, "I'm too young! I can't speak to the nations!" God made no apologies in correcting his words, "Say not I'm too young!" God knew that the more he spoke negative words, he would literally seal his destiny. Consequently, he changed the way he spoke, and it changed his future! (See Jeremiah 1)

By now, you realize that you have the ability to change the entire direction of your life with words. Your words can stop you from experiencing God's best in your life or they can propel you to enjoying everything He has prearranged for you to enjoy.

> YOUR DREAMS COULD BE DELAYED BECAUSE OF WHAT YOU'RE SAYING.
> —JOEL OSTEEN

We can learn more about someone by listening to the way they speak than by anything else. Your words are a telltale sign of what you thoroughly believe. If you really believe that God's Word is true and it is the final authority in your life, then pay close attention to His instructions concerning your future:

We are instructed to "declare the end from the beginning."
(See Isaiah 46:10)

We are advised to "declare new things before they happen."
(See Isaiah 42:9)

Based on personal experience, I want to give you three powerful keys to position you to live the very dreams on your vision board.

#1. Declare God's Promises Over Your Life

Declaring God's promises over your life is one of the most powerful things you can ever do. God's Word spoken out of your mouth is your enemy's worst nightmare! He cannot stand to hear positive, faith-filled words coming from your lips. Why? Because what you repeatedly hear, you will eventually believe. When you consistently hear uplifting, positive declarations spoken from your own mouth about your future, you will get in agreement with it, and eventually experience it!

The Word of God spoken from your mouth releases you from all those limiting beliefs and impossibilities in your head. Not only that, but we are told that angels actually hearken (or adhere to) the words spoken from our mouths. Imagine how

> IT'S ONE THING TO STOP SAYING THE WRONG THINGS, BUT YOU'VE GOT TO START SAYING THE RIGHT THINGS.
> —JOYCE MEYER

your life would improve if you consistently declared God's Word. I have listed some of my favorite scriptures to confess over my life.

Speaking the Word of God over your life and your future dreams and goals is crucial. Powerful Scriptures, made personal, to speak out of your mouth:

- "I will be strong and not give up, for my work will be rewarded." (See 2 Chronicles 15:7)
- "God is giving me the desires of my heart and making all my plans succeed." (See Psalm 20:4)
- "I delight myself in the Lord, and he will give me the desires of my heart." (See Psalm 37:4)
- "I trust in the Lord with all my heart and lean not on my own understanding; in all my ways, I acknowledge Him and He shall direct my path." (See Proverbs 3:5-6)
- "I commit to the Lord whatever I do, and he will establish my plans." (See Proverbs 16:3)
- "I do not remember the former things nor consider the things of old, behold, God is doing a new thing in my life and now it shall spring forth." (See Isaiah 43:18-19)
- "I can do all this through him who gives me strength." (See Philippians 4:13)
- "I will not throw away my confidence; it will be richly rewarded." (See Hebrews 10:35)
- "I throw off everything that hinders and the sin that so easily entangles me. I run with perseverance the race marked out for me, fixing my eyes on Jesus." (See Hebrews 12:1)
- "God gives strength to the weary and increases power to the weak." (See Isaiah 40:29)
- "I am strong in the Lord and in his mighty power."

(See Ephesians 6:10)
- "His grace is sufficient for me and strength is made perfect in weakness." (See 2 Corinthians 12:9)
- "God knows the plans He has for me, plans for welfare and not evil, to give me a future and a hope." (See Jeremiah 29:11)

#2. Declare Your Unique, Individual Desires

You must eliminate all the negative words that are trapping you into the very things you don't want and replace those words with positive declarations of where you want to be. Brian Tracy recommends using affirmations that are positive, present tense, and personal. Simply by changing the way you speak, you will improve your level of confidence, boost your self-esteem, increase your courage and see positive results unfold.

Back in 2007, I made a list of positive declarations to speak over myself every single morning. Here's a sample of some of my declaration list:

- I am disciplined in spirit, soul, and body.
- I am proactive.
- I am highly focused on my dreams and goals.
- I am confident.
- I am in the best physical shape of my life.
- I am highly organized.
- I am successful.
- I am a bestselling author.
- I am confident to speak on television.
- I am confident to speak to live audiences.
- I am wealthy.

- I attract God-inspired ideas that produce millions of dollars.
- I am an expert in the message God has given me to share.
- I am highly favored.
- I speak at the largest conferences in the world.
- I am full of joy.
- I am filled with peace.
- I have the mind of Christ.
- I am energetic.

Keep in mind, I began speaking most of these declarations "by faith" because the reality was quite the opposite. Over time, I began to cooperate with my confessions and literally watch the changes take place. When I walk out on stage preparing to speak to thousands of people, I am reminded, "I am confident to speak to live audiences" because I hear myself say this daily! Is it a coincidence that what I am *declaring* . . . I am *experiencing*?!

Know for a fact that you have angels assigned to respond to the words you speak out of your mouth. They are "on call" just waiting for you to speak faith-filled words. So, what are you waiting for? What do you want to see happen in your future? Whatever it is, speak it out!

- "I am debt-free."
- "I am promoted."
- "I am highly favored."
- "I am enjoying divine health in my body."
- "I am disciplined."
- "I am happily married."
- "I am gifted to communicate."
- "I am filled with peace."

#3. Declare Your Dreams

Some dreams will never manifest in your life until you begin speaking them out loud. Remember, take a proactive approach to your dreams! Speak them out *before* they happen!

- "I am a bestselling author."
- "I am leading a department."
- "I am the best fitness instructor."
- "I am completely debt-free."
- "I am pastoring the greatest church."
- "I am the top sales winner in our organization."

Do you want to see where your life is headed? Listen to the words that are coming out of your mouth. If you change what you're saying, you'll change what you're seeing.

ACTION STEP

#1. Make a list of positive declarations to speak over yourself. Begin your statements with the words I am. These are power words. Your spirit takes any sentence that begins with "I am" as a command. It is a directive to make happen.

#2. Structure your declaration in the present tense. State what you are expecting in the present tense as if it is already yours.

#3. State your dream in the positive. Always state your declarations in the positive form. Avoid the negative focus such as: "I'm losing weight." "I'm not in debt." Instead, say things such as: "I am debt-free." "I am at my perfect weight of 115 pounds."

#4. Speak them out consistently. Set an alarm on your phone (if needed) in order to develop this habit in your life. You will get to a place in your daily routine where you no longer need to be reminded, you just do it. The more you do it, the more you begin to memorize your declarations and they just start pouring out of your mouth.

The best way to start a habit is to do it at the same time each day. I recommend starting and ending your day speaking to your future. It doesn't take long; it just takes consistency.

Warning: simply reading words on a piece of paper or staring at a vision board and reading your dreams in a robotic tone is not going to change your circumstances. Yes, your words have power, but you must believe that what you're speaking is going to happen.

Your faith (your belief in God's ability) activates His power in your life. You are practicing what God instructed us to do in Mark 11:23-24 (NIV): "Truly I tell you, if anyone says to this mountain, 'Go, throw yourself into the sea,' and does not doubt in their heart but believes that what they say will happen, it will be done for them. Therefore I tell you, whatever you ask for in prayer, believe that you have received it, and it will be yours."

The responsibility is on you to believe it. The Apostle Paul said, "I believed, and therefore have I spoken." (2 Corinthians 4:13 KJV) Again, you must believe it. There is power in your mouth. Make a list of the positive changes you want to see in your life, and start speaking them out consistently.

SEVEN
THE LAW OF ATTRACTION IN ACTION
What Are You Currently Attracting?

> YOU GET IT WHEN YOU BELIEVE IT.
> —JIM CARREY

Many people get so caught up in list making and designing a "scrapbook on a corkboard" that they overlook a powerful principle from the Word of God.

When you change the way you look at things, the things you look at will change! Gratitude produces the law of attraction in action; furthermore, so does complaining.

In other words, as long as you complain about your current life, you will only attract more to complain about. The opposite is true as well; as long as you express gratitude for what you currently have, you will only attract more to be grateful for. Gratitude can instantly transform your life.

No matter where you are in life, you have something to be grateful for. As soon as you recognize it and express it, your life will start to improve. Your health, your career, your relationships, your finances, your opportunities— all of these are affected by your attitude of gratitude. Like attracts like.

Most people do not realize that focusing on what they do not have only causes them to attract never having it. When we find fault with and voice our complaints about our lives, we are actually creating an environment to receive more of what we are complaining about.

Using your mouth to express gratitude and voice your thankfulness is that one small change that can catapult you from wishing to experiencing your dreams. I have adapted this into my daily routine, and it has opened up a doorway of blessings, opportunities, favor and joy in my life like never before.

Remember, Proverbs 23:7 says we are what we think in our hearts. What you think about, you continue to bring about. If you dwell on poverty, never having enough, always missing opportunities, never succeeding, and always coming up short then that is exactly what will come to you.

When you use your mouth to express gratitude for what you already have, you have just opened the door for success. If you adopt the discipline of voicing gratitude rather than complaints, you will experience greater success in seeing your dreams realized.

Think for a moment about Christmastime. When your relatives show sincere appreciation and excitement over the gifts you give, you automatically want to shower them with more gifts. On the contrary, when recipients appear ungrateful, displeased, or unimpressed with your gift, you are less likely to give them a gift the next year or end up offering a small token out of a sense of obligation.

God also responds with greater generosity when we give verbal expressions of thanksgiving for all that He's done in your life, He is "champing at the bit" so-to-speak to give you more!

If you want to remain stressed out, in debt, out of shape,

on the verge of a divorce or a nervous breakdown, then continue to complain. That word itself actually means to remain. As Joyce Meyer candidly puts it, "Complain and remain."

That's exactly what happened to the Israelites. They griped, murmured, and complained about their lack of food, lack of new shoes, lack of abundance, etc. As a result, they remained circling a mountain for forty years when it should have only taken eleven days to pass into the Promised Land!

What conditions are you experiencing year after year with no progress? Are you complaining about your metabolism, your lazy spouse, your rebellious children, your lousy job, your inability to lose weight, your lingering debts, your low-paying job, etc. Does it appear that these circumstances have remained the same for a long period? Perhaps it has to do with voicing your complaints.

> GRATITUDE IS A POWERFUL PROCESS. THE ONLY WAY TO MOVE TO THE NEXT LEVEL IS YOU MUST SHOW GRATITUDE FOR WHERE YOU ARE. IF YOU SHOW GRATITUDE IT GETS YOU TO WHERE YOU WANT TO BE QUICKER.
> —STEVE HARVEY

On any given day, you will hear people complaining. Just do a little experiment for yourself. During your lunch break, listen to your co-workers. When you get home, listen to your children or your spouse. When you call your friends, listen to what's on their minds. When you stand in the grocery line, listen to the person behind you on their cell phone. We complain about nearly everything—how long it takes to check out at the store, how long the lines are, how slow the traffic is moving, how many commercials appear during our favorite show, how bad the weather is, how tired we are, how our head hurts, how much work we have to do, how we dread Mondays, how much weight we've gained, how tired we are of hearing complaints!

It's crazy how our world is so fast-paced. We work harder, have more than we ever had before; however, we appear more unhappy, disgruntled, overwhelmed, unhealthy, and somewhat depressed in the midst of it all. How do we get a hold of this?

"Be thankful and say so." (Psalm 100:4 AMP)

Notice the Bible does not say, "Be thankful and think so." We are clearly instructed to voice our gratitude and appreciation. Just as we cherish words of appreciation from our children and from those we give gifts to, God is no different. He likes simply being told, "Thank You, Lord." Get into a habit of literally saying out loud or quietly under your breath, "Thank You, Jesus," and say it for everything.

- Thank You for loving me.
- Thank You for forgiving me.
- Thank You for blessing my life.
- Thank You for being so faithful.
- Thank You for changing me.
- Thank You for giving me the desires of my heart.
- Thank You for my health.
- Thank You for my family.
- Thank You for my job.
- Thank You for my gifts and talents.
- Thank You for energy in my body.
- Thank You for renewing my youth.

- Thank You for restoring my soul.

You've probably been told most of your life to "count your blessings." Truly, when you express appreciation for what you already have, it multiplies.

Gratitude for Weight Loss

One of the ways we maintain our "less than desirable" bodies is through the words of our mouths. Complaining and constantly focusing on the negative viewpoints we have of ourselves causes us to remain that way.

- "I hate my thighs!"
- "My stomach is huge!"
- "I'll never get this weight off!"
- "No matter what I do, I can't lose weight."
- "This cellulite is disgusting!"

Whatever you focus on expands. The more you voice your dislike over your current physical condition, the more you dislike it. I experienced this years ago when my age reached a milestone and the loudest voices around me were claiming:

- "It's harder to lose weight when you reach forty."
- "You won't be able to eat like you did when you were thirty."
- "You have to work out twice as hard as you did when you were a teenager just to burn the same amount of calories."
- "You're about to reach the menopause stage and you'll gain weight."

I had always been a fairly petite woman with a pretty good metabolism, but I listened to those voices and started to believe them. Suddenly, I began to look in the mirror and really dislike my thighs, my hips, my waist, my face, everything! Overall, I felt larger than normal. Increasingly, I began to gain weight and develop a strong discouragement over my lack of ability to "look like my old self."

Strangely, I was eating healthier than ever and working out harder, but looking worse than ever. I was convincing myself that "no matter what I try, nothing is working!" Those are debilitating thoughts. The more I believed it and expressed it, the more it became my reality.

Finally, I began to get control of myself, my thoughts, my words, and my attitude. I found a photo of myself at my ideal weight wearing a bikini. I put it on my vision board (the one nobody saw but me) and began looking at it every single day. In prayer, I would close my eyes and imagine myself looking like that again. Literally, I visualized my thin thighs, my trim waist, my flat stomach, my slender face, everything. I wrote out clearly, "I am so happy weighing my perfect weight of 107-110 pounds."

I exchanged my complaints for positive declarations and expressions of gratitude such as:

- I am grateful for my fast metabolism.
- I am grateful that I am in the best physical shape of my life.
- I am grateful that I can eat what I want and maintain my perfect weight.
- I am grateful to be free from food and bondage to food.
- I am free from torment over my body.
- I am happy with my body.
- I am healthy and in excellent shape.

- I am thin, firm, and muscular.
- I am disciplined.
- I am full of energy.
- I enjoy working out.

Then I began thanking the Lord for His promises to me in the Word of God.

Thank You, Lord, according to Your Word:

- "The righteous cry out, and the Lord hears them, and delivers them from all their troubles. Thank you for delivering me from torment over my body." (See Psalm 34:17)
- "In the multitude of my anxieties within me, your comforts delight my soul. I am free from anxiety over my body." (See Psalm 94:19)
- "I can do all things through Christ who strengthens me." (See Philippians 4:13)
- "Your grace is sufficient for me. I have the grace to weigh what I want to weigh." (Grace means "the power of God coming on me to do with ease what I could never do on my own".) (See 2 Corinthians 12:9)
- "My body is the temple of the Holy Spirit. I choose to glorify You, Lord, in my body." (1 Corinthians 3:16)
- "I'm running hard for the finish line. I'm giving it everything I've got. No sloppy living for me! I'm staying alert and in top condition." (See 1 Corinthians 9:27)

Astoundingly, the weight began falling off of me. The struggle was over. I began to transform into the very image on that vision board. Since then, I have thoroughly guarded my words over my body. I do not complain over my thighs. I do not express frustration over the amount of calories I consumed. I do not deprive myself of something I want to eat. I expect to stay thin. I expect to maintain my ideal weight. I expect to have a high metabolism. And I constantly express gratitude to the Lord for giving me the desires of my heart.

What can you do to change your physical appearance? If you are dissatisfied with your current health or overall body image, start by deciding what you want to look like. If you have a photo of yourself when you looked your best, then that's the image you want to keep before your eyes.

Guard your mouth. What goes in your mouth isn't as important as what's coming out of it! Overeating is not nearly as detrimental to your weight goal as complaints are! Determine not to let one negative word come out of your mouth about your body again! I know it is not easy. We all have that tendency to look in the mirror and start to feel disgusted. Don't voice it. Your words are powerful and have a way of keeping you trapped in the very thing you don't want!

Trade all of those complaints for praise and thanksgiving for where you are headed. You are giving God something to work with. He responds to a grateful heart. He loves to hear your faith expressed through gratitude. All the reading of weight-loss books and purchasing of fitness equipment won't change a thing until you first guard your words.

Gratitude For Finances

Gratitude gives God an opportunity to restore and even multiply what's been stolen from you. A couple of years ago, I experienced what could have been a devastating financial setback of $11,000. Our daughter was attending a private school in Fort Worth, Texas where the tuition was $13,500 per year. It's a significantly steep price for high school tuition, but we were told of the school's credentials and college preparatory academy of excellence.

Kassidi was interviewed and given the "Leadership Scholarship" which reduced the tuition by $2,500. We were so grateful for the scholarship, which reduced our tuition cost to $11,000. I practiced what I have been teaching throughout this book. I printed a photo of the school's logo with the amount $11,000 typed across it and placed it on my vision board.

Each time I had extra finances, I would apply it toward our vision of paying cash for her tuition. Little by little we had the full amount and I proudly wrote out the check, sent it off, and marked it off my vision board!

Completely caught off guard, we were placed in an unfortunate situation with some volunteer faculty and one teacher who had very strong agendas against the "Christian girls" in a particular sport, my daughter, Kassidi, being one of them. They were set and determined to punish them and belittle them in front of the others time and time again.

Never had we experienced anything like that. Kassidi has always been so likable and easy-going and doesn't force her beliefs on anyone. It was the first and only time I ever had to call a meeting with the principal to find out why other moms were approaching me to say, "They are very degrading to your daughter."

Heartbroken and shocked, we prayed over what to do and after meeting with the principal, the disrespectful teachers and the Head Master, we felt it was time to quietly transition out of that situation and enroll in another school.

Even though Kassidi had only attended for two weeks, they kept the full $11,000 tuition! I was devastated! My husband was irate!

The Head Master said, "It saddens me that you can't be refunded the money, but you signed the contract!"

I had a choice. I could complain about what they basically stole from us. (After all, it was their unprofessional attitudes that forced us to leave the school.) And people encouraged me to take it to the Board of Directors, demand our money back, file a lawsuit, and even go to the local news station. Or I could turn it around and say, "Lord, Your Word says that if the thief be caught, he must pay back seven times what was stolen!" (See Proverbs 6:31) I might add that, honestly, Satan is the thief, not that school or that Head Master, and he always has an agenda to steal, kill and destroy. So, I chose to trust God's Word that somehow, some way, God would restore seven times what Satan (the thief) stole from us.

My dad, Jerry Savelle, wrote a bestselling book years ago titled, *If Satan Can't Steal Your Joy, He Can't Keep Your Goods*. This book has changed hundreds of thousands of lives by this simple principle: turn your complaints into praise and watch what God can do!

I crossed out my $11,000 goal next to the school logo and wrote: $77,000! I never contacted the school and complained. I simply praised God for restoring to me seven times what was stolen! I thanked the Lord joyfully for $77,000 in my savings account!

I set the $77,000 goal on September 6th and by August 16th—eleven months later, I had received $77,500 from unexpected, additional income aside from my regular paycheck! God actually went over and above my goal and it didn't even take a year!

Which would you rather have? Your $11,000 check refunded with a disgruntled attitude? Or a grateful, forgiving attitude and $77,000 deposited into your savings account?

Gratitude Gives God an Opportunity to Show Off!

Wealth "experts" actually suggest that if you want to increase your financial wealth, start focusing on being more grateful. The idea behind it is that by expressing feelings of gratitude, you'll literally feel more wealthy and thereby attract more abundance into your life.

This is more than just "looking on the bright side." When you begin expressing gratitude, especially when your circumstances are less than pleasant, you're likely to begin trying your best to say things such as:

- I'm grateful that at least I have a roof over my head.
- I'm grateful that at least I have food to eat.
- I'm grateful that at least I have a job.
- I'm grateful that at least I have a car.
- I'm grateful that at least I'm healthy.
- I'm grateful that at least I have a vacation, etc.

All of these "at least" expressions are an attempt to build some sort of positive momentum, but genuinely deep down, you're not that thrilled about it. When you get a deep revelation of how powerful your expressions of praise, thanksgiving, and gratitude are, your circumstances become irrelevant because you know they're about to change in your favor.

Gratitude means you stop focusing on what you don't have and start focusing on what you do have. It is one of the most positive emotions we have.

Vital Key: You Must Feel It!

This is so vital that I had to use it as a heading to make you really see it. You absolutely must feel as if you already have what you pinned on that vision board! That means fists clinched, wide smiled, squealing with exhilaration because you know that it's done! Your dreams are en route to your house! I remember being in so many church services where the minister would say, "How would you express your praise to God if He answered your prayer right this minute?" The church would erupt in extravagant praise and thanksgiving! Then, the minister would say, "Then, go ahead and show Him what you believe."

When you praise God with that much enthusiasm, it gets His attention. He sees your faith! Identify how you would feel if your dream manifested today. If you think you can't fake that feeling, then you're still not convinced that you can have it.

"If you believe in your heart, and do not doubt in your mind."
—Mark 11:23-24

The 24-Hour Test

In order to launch this attitude of gratitude, I want you to embark on a full day of expressing your heartfelt gratitude for everything. This also means no complaining whatsoever. Do not complain that you woke up late; don't complain about the weather, the traffic, the bad hair day, the nuisance of having to get gas, the frequent red lights, the co-workers popping in your office, the baby crying all night, the hassle of cooking, the deadline that's coming up, the soccer game you must attend, your life in general. No complaints for twenty-four hours.

For an entire day start saying, "Thank You, Lord" for anything and everything. The moment you open your eyes, thank the Lord for the new day. Thank the Lord for the food in your refrigerator, your closet full of clothing, the bed you slept in, and the roof over your head. After all, you're doing better than 75% of the world's population.[45] When you open the refrigerator door and "can't find anything to eat," thank the Lord for the pleasure of getting to eat three meals a day. You're better off than one billion people on the planet who might get to eat once a day. Thank the Lord for your job and think about those who are unemployed month after month. Thank the Lord for your health as you think about those waking up again in a hospital bed. Thank the Lord for your computer or your phone and its ability to connect you with friends and family all over the world.

You will be utterly amazed at how a simple shift in your attitude from complaining to expressing gratitude can bring such fulfillment, absolute relief from stress and anxiety, appearance of blessings, an atmosphere of peace, the presence of God, strength in your body, and the realization of your dreams.

The Highest Expression of Your Faith

Now, take it a step further and start thanking God in advance for what He is about to do in your life.

This is the highest expression of your faith. This offering of praise and thanksgiving for what you are desiring touches the heart of God. It shows Him just how much you trust Him. It communicates that you really believe He loves you.

Consider the example of Paul and Silas. (See Acts 16:16-40) When they were in prison and began boldly and loudly worshiping God for His faithfulness, proclaiming how awesome and powerful He is; and they were still shackled to the wall of a jail cell. They had been arrested. They had been beaten. They were bruised, battered, and in pain. They were imprisoned with no hope of ever getting out. But their faith-filled words of praise and thanksgiving put God on the move. He sent an earthquake from heaven that shook the building. The walls began to crumble, the prison doors opened up, the chains fell off of them, and they walked out of there free as could be.

This supernatural event would never have happened had these two men of God not spoken their faith out loud. They had to give voice to their belief in and devotion to God. Your life will never change until you begin vocalizing what you believe God intends to do for you and through you. When you praise and thank God, you are activating your faith and doing exactly what God's Word tells you to do.

The Power of Praise

Verbally expressing your gratitude and praise create an atmosphere where God begins to work. Remember, the Bible is full of stories of people bowing down and worshiping God before they got their breakthrough. Worship Him first and foremost on your journey to fulfill your vision. Don't thank Him after your dreams come true and you reach your goals. Sure, it's easy to thank somebody after they've done something nice for you. But thanking God before you see results shows Him that you wholeheartedly believe in the vision He has given you and that you are going to give it everything you've got.

You may have tried this in the past and gotten discouraged. You may be thinking, *Terri, I have been worshiping God that I'm free from debt, that my bills are paid and that I have money in the bank, but nothing has changed.* I know it might be hard and it requires a lot of faith, especially when the natural dictates the opposite of what you believe; but you've got to do it. And you've got to *keep* doing it.

If you are on the verge of giving up right now, be encouraged that you are close to victory. You are close to your dream. My dad believes that feeling as if you have no choice but to quit is always an indication that your breakthrough is right around the corner. Don't give up. Determine in your heart that no matter how impossible your dreams may look at this very moment, you will hang in there.

Paul wrote, "For in due season we shall reap, if we faint not." (Galatians 6:9 KJV) Persevering when things get tough is a long-term commitment. You don't try to dig in your heels to see how it goes. You can't treat it like a test run where if you don't get results immediately, you go back to your old ways. You must determine that you will not quit. You will not give up. You will faint not and reap your dreams.

What are you thankful for? My dad says, "The depth of your praise determines the magnitude of your breakthrough." Being grateful is a habit you must practice regularly. Get into the routine of thanking God for anything and everything. Using the gratitude journal section of your *Dream It. Pin It. Live It. Workbook*, take some time and think about ten things for which you are grateful. Include things you are enjoying right now and dreams and desires that have not yet come to pass. Write them all down. When you are done making your list, tell God out loud how thankful you are for His past, present, and future provisions and for the manifestations in your life.

Act the Part

If you really believe you receive when you pray, then go ahead and take it a step further, and act the part! Talk like a person who has already achieved their dream. Walk confidently like a person who has attained success. Dress like a person who lives the life you desire to live. This demonstration of faith will create positive expectancy at a whole new level.

Journal Your Gratitude

Why is it so important that you write down what you're grateful for? Keeping a gratitude journal positions you to naturally start looking for things to appreciate, which, in turn, only causes you to attract more to be grateful for. It really is that simple.

When I moved my headquarters in 2014, I felt impressed to open my weekly staff meetings with gratitude. I initiated the first meeting by distributing little sticky notepads around the table to my team. I said, "Write down a few things you're grateful for since we moved here." They began writing. One-by-one, we move around the table reading from our notes, voicing our gratitude for all God has done. You can't help but be encouraged by the atmosphere produced by this simple procedure. Some team members remembered things others forgot. Others recognized little things some didn't even think of. I told them to share as big or as small as they want. Nothing is insignificant. We have so much to be grateful for. They began sharing things such as:

- "All the new people we met in Boston last week at

the conference."
- "Our YouTube subscribers have already doubled in a couple months!"
- "Our new book release."
- "That I get to work with the greatest team members here!"
- "We received the largest donation we've ever received."
- "This testimony of a fourteen-year old girl who stopped cutting herself after hearing our messages."
- "The forty people we prayed with at the altar last Wednesday night."
- "The invitation this week to speak at a new success conference."
- "The environment we get to work in."

The gratitude is endless. Here's the key: Since that day, we haven't stopped; but we also have never lacked for something to be grateful for! Week after week, we open each team meeting with thankfulness. Not one time have we been speechless. Consistently, we are overwhelmed at how much we have to be grateful for just since the previous meeting!

Personally, I kept a gratitude journal for thirty days, and I want you to see what took place in my life during this quick month of journaling:

- My daughter had been praying for a modeling job for five months, and she got the job!
- A friend who had been struggling with drug and alcohol addiction for years, started rehab and is now free from substance abuse (after twenty years of struggling)!

- Our ministry received more charitable donations in this single month than any month previously!! (Donations of $50,000, $15,000, $10,000, $5,000)
- I was unexpectedly blessed with the finances to pay cash for our family vacation!
- A family member was healed.
- A relationship in my life was supernaturally restored.
- My daughter got accepted to the university she was praying to get into.
- Significant increase in our ministry outreach and exposure occurred.
- I was given a $1,500 pair of designer shoes!!!
- I was invited to speak at a success conference to 14,000 entrepreneurs.

All in thirty days! I didn't do this just for an experiment. I journaled my gratitude because I wanted to express my heart to the Lord and be mindful of what He is doing in my life. But, gratitude opens the door for God to do even more. I am living proof.

Start your new routine of journaling 5-10 things you're grateful for each day for thirty days. They don't have to be enormous, breakthrough occurrences—those rarely happen on a daily basis. It can be as simple as:

- "I am so grateful for the home I live in."
- "I am so grateful for the neighborhood I can walk in."
- "I am so grateful for the peace in my mind."
- "I am so grateful for my precious children."
- "I am so grateful that God forgives me."
- "I am so grateful for my health."

Watch what God will do in the life of a grateful heart!

ACTION STEP

Set aside time to journal your gratitude for the things that have happened and for what you are believing will come in the future.

EIGHT

DON'T SHARE BIG DREAMS WITH SMALL MINDS

Who Should See Your Dreams?

> SO ENCOURAGE EACH OTHER AND
> BUILD EACH OTHER UP, JUST
> AS YOU ARE ALREADY DOING.
> —1 THESSALONIANS. 5:11 [NIV]

Your success can be determined in part by those with whom you surround yourself, but it can also be determined by those you do *not* have around you. Small-minded people have a way of sucking ambition right out of you. Big minds have a way of elevating you to reach your highest potential.

One of the most important decisions we make in life is choosing our friendships. Who you share your dreams with makes a difference in your ability to achieve those dreams. After all, when Joseph announced his big dream to his own family, they wanted to kill him. You might need to keep your mouth closed around certain people, perhaps even your closest family members.

Who you spend your time with has a huge impact on the dreams you achieve. God will strategically place people in your life to inspire you to rise higher. Your enemy, Satan, will also strategically place people in your life to pull you down. Choose your associations wisely.

If you spend time with someone who has cold or flu symptoms, you'll most likely catch what they have. If you invest most of your time with people who cause you to compromise, think small, and limit your potential, you will forfeit the dreams God has put in your heart. I've heard it said that if you want to see where your life will be over the next five years, look at the list of names in your cell phone. You become like those you spend the most time with.

This tendency can be seen (and heard) in someone who moves to another country. Over time, they tend to pick up on the accent spoken in their new foreign home. Little by little, you can hear a change in their pronunciation of words.

You are who you associate with. If you have friends who are generous, excellent in their appearance, live by a higher standard, and believe all things are possible with God, then you will rise to that level. At the same time, if you have friends who are unmotivated, negative, and content with where they are, you'll begin to imitate their behavior.

We all need to make assessments of the people we are spending most of our time with and how they may be affecting our lives. Now, I'm not suggesting that you just start cutting your friends and family out of your life because they have small dreams. I am recommending that you consider what type of impact their relationship has on your pursuit of what God has put in your heart.

In reference to your big dreams and your list of goals, do your current close associations support these pursuits? Will they laugh at your vision board? Will they snicker and sarcastically reply, "In your dreams!"? Will they show disinterest in your ambitions because they think it's a waste of time and those types of dreams don't happen to "people like us"?

If so, you need to consider distancing yourself or diminishing your time allocated to these types of associations. "Misery loves company," as the saying goes. People who have accepted a lower standard of living and think dreaming is foolish will not aid or support your new realization. Do what you can to communicate encouragement with them, but if they choose to remain where they are, then you have a decision to make.

I am not necessarily suggesting total abandonment (unless you feel that is vital), but distancing yourself to a degree and limiting your exposure to their negativity will only help you. There are some things you cannot tolerate any longer if you're truly going to run after these long-awaited dreams. Their pessimistic outlook on your future will bleed you dry of energy and make it impossible for you to reach your full potential.

Nothing gets you off course faster than staying with the wrong crowd. You cannot live a successful life if you're allocating all of your energy and focus on trying to convince others that your dreams aren't crazy. In some cases, you need to put your foot down and walk away.

If you've ever had a friend or relative in prison or even visited a prison, you will quickly discover from the stories of the inmates that they have a common thread. One by one, they were affected by their environment, their community, their associations. Bottom line: their relationships led to trouble. From hanging around gang members, drug addicts, and thieves, they became like those they were around the most.

You can take control over the influences in your life. You can choose your connections based on people you admire, respect, and want to resemble. If you're ready to go after the big dreams and goals God has put in your heart, then it's also time to take a close look at the people who surround you. Are your closest friends holding you back? Do they want more out of life? Do they have a poor mentality? Do they reject personal growth and development? Do they feel as if they paid their dues by finishing school and have no interest in ever learning another thing? Basically, do they feel like they've learned all they need to learn to get by? Do your friends have dreams, goals, and aspirations to do more or are they content to settle where they are?

As you grow, enlarge your thinking and develop greater ambition. You will start to feel terribly unattached and uncomfortable around your old associations. Immediately, you'll recognize your vocabulary is different, your outlooks are contrary, your topics of discussion are incompatible. Why? You have changed. You've grown. You want more out of life. You know God wants you to expand, increase, enlarge your capacity to dream.

> THERE JUST AREN'T ENOUGH HOURS IN THE DAY TO WASTE TIME INTERACTING WITH PEOPLE WHO ARE NOT FOCUSED, DRIVEN AND IN SOME WAY HELPING YOU ACHIEVE YOUR GOALS.
> —NIGEL BOTTERILL

Who does not need to see your vision board:

#1. Negative Thinkers
Those who are pessimistic in their outlook or who find only problems and no solutions. They are not able to get past what looks difficult to see what can be.

#2. Sleepwalkers
Those who've settled for mediocrity are what I would

describe as sleepwalkers. They lack focus in their lives and are content to work, eat, sleep, repeat. They are on autopilot with their every day lives and do not see beyond today. As Pastor Joel Sims puts it, "If you never think beyond today, then what is tomorrow destined to look like? A carbon copy of today." Might as well sleepwalk through life.

#3. Negative talkers
You do have control over what you say about your future, but you do not have control over what others say. Rather than have to consciously eliminate their negative, doubt-filled words from replaying in your head, just avoid sharing your dreams with them altogether. Some words are poisonous and can take time in not allowing them to take root in your heart.

#4. Gossipers
Successful people never worry about what others are doing. Success-driven people do not waste their time talking about other people. They are too focused on achieving their own dreams to bother themselves with mindless chatter.

#5. Dream thieves
These are people who don't contribute to or support your dreams. Whether they put you and your dreams down or they tell you you'll never achieve them, they are robbing you of motivation, encouragement, and excitement.

Intentional Friendships

Since who you spend time with influences who you become, you may need some new relationships in your life. If you invest your time with successful, positive-minded friends, you will become a more proactive goal-achiever. Period.

> *"If you walk with wise men, you'll become wise.*
> *But the companion of fools will be destroyed."*
> —*(Proverbs 13:20 paraphrased)*

You will shape your future by choosing to spend time with people you aspire to be like. You must be very selective about your associations. Their habits, good or bad, tend to rub off on you. The activities you engage in, the books you read, the movies you watch, and the people you choose to interact with all influence your life and shape your identity.

If you are surrounded by people who haven't grown in years and they are content with staying at the level they're on, then you won't see any need for growth in your life. However, you get around people who are investing in themselves, attending conferences, listening to audio messages, reading books, discussing their next plan, excited about their future, then you'll get on the bandwagon with them. We see this in sports when a ballplayer improves after being placed on a better team with better peers. People rise to the level of their positive surroundings.

Connect with people who have skills and qualities that you admire and want to emulate in your life. Yes, it requires more confidence and may be a bit uncomfortable to sur- round yourself with quality people, but that means you're growing. As long as you're comfortable, you're not growing.

If you're at the head of the class, then that means you're not learning anything. When you stop learning, you stag- nate. You stop making progress. On purpose, get around people who make you feel a little awkward and uneasy because they are smarter, more educated, more successful, more financially wealthy, etc. Just by getting around people who are inspiring, optimistic, driven, disciplined, and highly motivated, you will "catch" their qualities.

Success Is Contagious

The company you keep reflects your personality. Who you choose to surround yourself with speaks of your values. You are the mirror reflection of your influencers.

> IT IS BETTER TO BE ALONE THAN IN THE WRONG COMPANY. TELL ME WHO YOUR BEST FRIENDS ARE AND I WILL TELL YOU WHO YOU ARE. IF YOU RUN WITH WOLVES, YOU WILL LEARN HOW TO HOWL BUT IF YOU ASSOCIATE WITH EAGLES, YOU WILL LEARN HOW TO SOAR TO GREAT HEIGHTS.
> —JOHN MASON

Want to be successful? Surround yourself with successful people.

I read a story about a man who went from rags to riches after deciding to change his friendships. He looked around at his closest friendships and noticed that they equally hated hard work and had no intention or desire to improve themselves.

Out of curiosity, he asked a very wealthy man, who wasn't any more talented or more educated than he was, how he was able to become a millionaire. The wealthy man simply said, "Keep the right company." So, he did. He followed that

> GET COMFORTABLE BEING UNCOMFORTABLE: THAT'S HOW YOU BREAK THE PLATEAU AND REACH THE NEXT LEVEL.
> —CHALENE JOHNSON

> IF YOU'RE AT THE HEAD OF THE CLASS, YOU'RE IN THE WRONG CLASS.
> —JOHN MAXWELL

advice by attending conventions and seminars to connect with people who wanted more out of life.

As he began making connections with these new goal-oriented people, he decided to make a list. The list was really simple. One column was for those who would improve the quality of his life and the other column was for those who would drag him down.

If an individual on the list could improve his life, he would spend as much time around them as possible. If someone could drag him down, he limited his time to no more than five minutes around them. After following his "make or break" list, he became a millionaire within three years!

I read where Thomas Edison, Harvey Firestone, and Henry Ford had winter homes in Fort Meyers, Florida. In fact, Edison and Ford purchased homes next door to each other. These men were all very successful in their own field of expertise, and they chose to associate closely with each other.[46]

I also discovered that American author, Pulitzer Prize and Nobel Prize winner, Ernest Hemingway had close associations with other up-and-coming writers. Their network helped influence each other and drove each other to write every single day. They challenged each other to continue perfecting their craft and improving their skills.

Each of those close friends produced historic works of literature including: F. Scott Fitzgerald (author of *The Great Gatsby*), Virginia Woolf (author of *To the Lighthouse*) and James Joyce (author of *Ulysses*).

Aristotle Onassis advised recent graduates to live in the best neighborhood in the most supportive city for the sake of their personal and professional lives. "Even if you have to take a room in the attic," said Onassis. He was convinced that you would absorb the lifestyle and mindset of the environment by osmosis; and thereby, rise to its level.

So, Who Are Your "Five"?

If you are the average of the five people you spend the most time with, then don't settle for average people. What would that say about you? Look for people who are focused and determined. Cling to their enthusiasm for life. Learn from their skillset. Allow them to push you to a higher level.

Seek out relationships with people who have qualities you desire. Until you establish a strong network of like-minded dreamers, you need to launch your personal growth by connecting with people you admire from afar. Listen to their audio teachings, read their books and manuals for success, attend their conferences and speaking engagements, watch their online videos or subscribe to their podcasts. Absorb as much information as you can until you begin to grow into the person you want to become.

Just as you become like the people you spend the most time with, you also transform into those you spend the most time listening to and learning from. Being exposed to their teaching is similar to interacting with them.

I love when I meet people who say to me, "Terri, I feel like I know you. You ride in the car with me every day to work;" or, "I work out with you every day;" or "You put me to sleep every night." (Honestly, I'm not sure how I feel about that one!) All joking aside, that is exactly how I transformed my thinking years ago and began dreaming bigger through the exposure of other big dreamers by audio recordings and books.

Be selective about your closest associations. Choose, on purpose, to surround yourself with greatness and you, too, will become great.

> YOU ARE THE AVERAGE OF THE FIVE PEOPLE YOU SPEND THE MOST TIME WITH.
> —JIM ROHN

ACTION STEP

Make a list of the five people (closest friends) who surrounded you:

1.)

2.)

3.)

4.)

5.)

Identify at least one quality you admire most about each one.

1.)

2.)

3.)

4.)

5.)

On a scale of 1-10, how would you rate their ambition?

1.)

2.)

3.)

4.)

5.)

NINE
WHAT TO DO WHILE YOU'RE WAITING
Successful People Have Successful Habits

> SUCCESS IS SOMETHING YOU ATTRACT
> BY THE PERSON YOU BECOME.
> —JIM ROHN

I recently heard that Warren Buffet was attending a dinner party with Bill Gates and Bill Gates, Sr. in Seattle. Bill Gates, Sr. asked the two men (who are among the five richest men in the world) what they think is the most important skill for success.

They both turned to him and said the same word simultaneously, "Focus!"[47]

What do you do while you are waiting patiently for these dreams and goals to manifest in your life? What do you do when time is ticking and it appears that nothing is changing? How do you stay optimistic in spite of what doesn't seem to be happening? You focus. "Focus on what?" you ask. Focus on a personal development plan.

In Chapter 3, I shared how Darren Hardy (editor of *Success* magazine) has interviewed the most successful people of our day, (Howard Shultz of Starbucks, Richard Branson,

Steve Jobs, Oprah Winfrey, Jeff Bezos, Joel Osteen, etc.) and related his observation that the common thread among them is their commitment to learning and having specific goals and a plan.

In Chapter 3, the focus was on clearly defining goals, but now I want you to notice how they also have a personal development plan. Before you get overwhelmed by that statement and think this is just another "self-help" book, I want you to see the simplicity in this idea. You change yourself by changing something you do each day. How do you change and develop into the person you desire to be? You change your routine.

Do you know that just by observing someone on a day-to-day basis, you can tell how successful they intend to become? No matter what day it is, just by simply taking note of the rituals and routines they adhere to on a consistent basis reveals where they are headed in life. It also communicates if you are headed closer to or further from your own dreams.

The Secret of Your Future Is in Your Daily Routine

Years ago, the late Jim Rohn was being mentored by a very wealthy man named Earl Shoaf. Mr. Shoaf made a strong statement to Jim one day that eventually altered his entire outlook on life, and I believe it will make a profound impact on yours, as well.

Mr. Shoaf said, "Jim, what you have at this moment, you have attracted by the person you've become!" Strong words, but that wasn't all. He went on to say, "If you don't have much, perhaps you haven't become much."

Obviously offended by such a remark, Jim held up his paycheck and matter-of-factly uttered, "This is all they pay!"

Mr. Shoaf responded, "No. This is all they pay YOU!"

The hard truth continued as Mr. Shoaf went on to say, "Don't they pay others five times this amount in your organization?"

"Yes," Jim answered.

"If you were to qualify for five times this amount, wouldn't your paycheck be five times this amount?"

Then, Mr. Shoaf added these life-changing comments:

- "If you were to develop better skills, you'll earn better income!"
- "The key is to become more valuable by changing you!"
- "Don't wish it was easier, wish you were better.
- "Don't wish for less problems, wish for more skills."[48]

As if those profound statements aren't enough to elevate your thinking, this one is the philosophy that says it all: "Learn to work harder on yourself than you do on your job. If you work hard on your job, you'll make a living. If you work hard on yourself, you can make a fortune!"

Wow! If you really take those words to heart, I am telling you from personal experience, you will change your entire life. You will walk toward the very dreams you have pasted on your vision board. You will see impossibilities become possible right before your eyes.

The Bible says, "To whom much is given, much is required." If you simply rearrange that very same scripture, you could say, "Much is required in order for much to be given."

The bottom line is this, if you want more, you must become

more. Your life will only grow to the extent that you grow. If you don't like the size of your life, make an investment in the size of you. Grow into the dreams you have.

Who Do You Need to Become to Achieve Your Goal?

What you achieve isn't nearly as important as *who* you become as you're working on a worthy goal. As you're working on a goal, the goal is working on you. This entire book is worth that statement.

The most ignorant declaration I made when I graduated from Texas Tech University was, "I will never study again!" Why? I concluded that I had "paid my dues" by studying for four years and graduating with honors. I believed I knew all I needed to know to start my future.

Well, for eleven years after my college graduation, I lived up to my ignorant promise. I was a ghostwriter, editing and writing over twenty-five books for other authors. I worked hard; I worked late; I worked nights when needed. I was fully vested in the organization and wanted to do the best job possible!

> THE PERSON WHO STOPS STUDYING MERELY BECAUSE THEY HAVE FINISHED SCHOOL IS FOREVER HOPELESSLY DOOMED TO MEDIOCRITY, NO MATTER WHAT THEIR CALLING.
> —NAPOLEON HILL

At the same time, I was "working hard on my job," I lived paycheck to paycheck, had a total of $1,000 in my savings account (after eleven years of employment), nothing in investments, paid my credit card bill every month, paid my car note every month, and everything about my life was average.

One morning in 2002, I decided to go to work on myself harder than I did on my job. Literally, everything changed. I went from ghostwriting books to authoring books. I went from attending conferences to speaking at conferences. I went from watching television for hours to co-hosting a TV show. My income more than tripled. My savings goals were reached. My investment portfolio grew. What happened?

I focused on a personal development plan by making a few, small changes in my daily routine. I am thoroughly convinced that if you change your routine, you can change your whole life. No, it doesn't happen in a day, but it all starts with one day.

Successful People Never Stop Growing

In his teaching on motivation, Zig Ziglar shares that Mary Kay Ashe of Mary Kay Cosmetics told him she never got in her car without a cassette that she could listen to while driving. He also said that billionaire H.L. Hunt listened to cassette recordings until after he was eighty years old and Wallace Johnson, the co-founder of Holiday Inns International listened to messages every day and read two good books every month even in his eighties. Alan Bean—one of the astronauts who walked on the moon—told Ziglar that on their way to the moon and back, they also listened to motivational teachings.[49]

These successful people represent the most goal-oriented people in the world, and they found it helpful to consistently listen to motivational teaching.

Habit #1 - Focus On Listening

What do you do while you are waiting for your dreams to manifest? In three words, build your faith.

"Faith comes by hearing and hearing by the Word of God."
—*Romans 10:17*

The first habit to adapt into your new routine is the habit of listening to faith-building, motivational teaching. This very well could be the missing ingredient you need to see your dreams come to pass. The Bible reveals to us that when we are born again, we accept Jesus as the Lord of our lives, we are instantly given the measure of faith. Each of us is given the exact same measure of faith. I was not given more than anyone else. Joel Osteen wasn't given more than you, nor Billy Graham or whomever you consider a person of great faith. It is distributed fairly.

Being given the measure of faith is no different from each us of being given the same number of muscles at birth. If that is the case and everything is given evenly and fairly, then why do some people have bulging, vein-popping, eye-catching muscles, and others have flab? The answer is clear, one has developed his muscles and the other has neglected theirs.

It is the same principle with faith. You may know someone who believes for millions of dollars and receives it while another person is only believing to fill up their car with gas. What is the difference? One has simply developed their faith (muscle) to a high degree and the other hasn't.

You need faith to achieve your dreams. The question becomes, "How can I increase my faith?" Refer back to Romans 10:17 and the answer is clear: faith comes by hearing. When I discovered how vital and how simple this key is to fulfilling my dreams, I became a woman on a quest to build my faith as quickly and as intently as possible. I did not want to waste another eleven years of my life with underdeveloped faith.

Building your faith is a choice just as with building your muscles. God gives you the choice to remain where you are or develop the kind of faith that can move mountains. Just as that bodybuilder with developed muscles can handle more weight than the guy who rarely lifts, you can develop your faith to such a degree that you will simply believe nothing is impossible with God!

The more your faith grows and develops, the more you can handle! As you listen to a faith-building message, faith grows! That's pretty simple, isn't it? At the same time, just as faith comes by hearing, faith goes by not hearing.

This practice of building your faith needs to be incorporated into your daily routine. Your faith level has to rise to meet your dream level. In fact, I believe you can tell a person's faith level by the dreams they are pursuing. Notice our foundational scripture says, "Faith comes by hearing and hearing." This implies that our practice of hearing the Word of God is in the continual present tense. We need to think of it as routinely as we do brushing our teeth.

Let's Not Waste Any More Time

Studies have shown that the average American watches more than five hours of television every single day. That means by the time you are sixty years old, you will have wasted fifteen years of your life glued to a box! Or, as I like to say, watching other people pursue their dreams. The average American is watching television shows they have no interest in anyway. The average person sleeps thirty minutes too late every day. [50] The average person, 18-34 years old, spends nearly four hours per day on social media! [51]

If you're desperate for change, you'll take desperate steps to change. This fundamental adjustment in my life has produced more of my dreams than I can even explain.

Entrepreneur magazine conducted research involving the habits of the wealthy versus the poor. They were looking for commonalities in their habits to see what they shared in order to become so successful. In this study, they defined "wealthy" as anyone earning at least $160,000/year with $3.2 million in assets. They defined "poor" as anyone earning under $30,000/year with less than $5,000 in assets. Here is what the study showed:

- Wake up 3+ hours before work = 44% wealthy/3% poor
- Listen to audio books during their commute = 63% wealthy/5% poor
- Read 30+ minutes or more each day = 88% wealthy/2% poor
- Exercise 4 days/week = 76% wealthy/23% poor
- Watch reality TV = 7% wealthy/78% poor
- Believe good habits create opportunity = 84% wealthy/4% poor [52]

The bottom line is that successful people have adopted successful habits. The first habit I want to introduce to you at this point in your vision board journey is simply the routine of listening to a faith-building, motivational teaching every day.

Notice that 63% of the "wealthy" people researched practiced the simple habit of listening to audio teachings during their commutes. Research has shown that the average person has an hour commute for work each day. Over a five-year period that is 1,250 hours in your car, and that's enough time to obtain the equivalent of a college education! The successful attend "automobile university."[53]

You can actually get to a place in your life where you enjoy traffic jams. Why? Because you're growing, your faith is increasing, and your fears are minimizing as you listen to uplifting teaching!

If the average American covers 12,000 miles per year in their automobile, that is the equivalent of spending 300 hours behind the wheel.[54] Do you think your faith would be larger if you listened to 300 hours of teaching? When you look at your vision board on the wall displaying so many impossible-looking dreams and goals, will you respond with fear or faith? It depends on what you are feeding the most. If you have 300 hours of faith-building teaching deposited inside your spirit, you will respond with great faith.

It's Impossible to Please God Without Faith

You are speaking the language of God when you respond with faith. How can you develop more faith? Faith comes by hearing. I want this so ingrained in your heart that you refuse to go another day without doing something to grow, increase, and make an investment in your faith.

> IF YOU WANT TO BE SUCCESSFUL, STUDY SUCCESSFUL PEOPLE. IF YOU WANT TO BE RICH, STUDY RICH PEOPLE. IF YOU WANT TO BE SKINNY, STUDY SKINNY PEOPLE.
> —DAVE RAMSEY

Back in 2002, I developed a hunger for more of God and

more of His will in my life. I was tired of living each year
with no progress, no goals and no vision for my life. I simply
purchased a CD player, borrowed some of my parents' audio
teachings from their collection, and wrote, "Push Play" on a
sticky note and attached it to my bathroom mirror.

I was endeavoring to start a new discipline in my life.
I had no idea that this simple act of pushing "Play" would
alter the rest of my life. My goal was this: "I'm going to listen
to a motivational message for twenty-one days." At the end
of that 21-day personal challenge, I didn't want to stop. I
wanted to complete a full month. At the end of thirty days,
I put a demand on myself to go for two months. That was in
2002, and I haven't stopped.

Here's the fundamental principle: As you listen to
faith-building words, something begins to change on the
inside of you. Your faith begins to grow. Your love for God
develops. Your belief in His mercy on your life expands. Your
acknowledgement of His plan for you personally increases.
Your dreams enlarge.

Develop your own plan for personal growth by starting
with a routine of listening. Experts suggest that you must
listen to something sixteen times for it to finally take root.
I can promise you this, at the end of twenty-one days, you
won't be the same person you are today. In addition, as you
make this simple change in your routine, you are developing a winning lifestyle.

Habit #2 - Focus On Reading

Zig Ziglar told an inspiring story about a guy named
Vince Robert who drove for a taxi cab company. Roberts,
from Ottawa, Canada, had achieved a 7th grade education
and began driving taxis for a living. At the age of thirty-

seven years old, he decided he was ready to make a change. Whether he acknowledged it or not, Vince Roberts began to focus on a personal development plan.

He simply walked into a bookstore, bought a 20 lb. *Webster's Dictionary,* and set a goal for himself to begin reading. He placed this heavy book on the front seat of his taxi, and while he waited for customers, he began with page one. He began to learn and memorize the meanings of words he had only heard before.

As he began practicing this new routine, he began to develop an appetite for learning. He wanted to know more. He began to grow and develop himself. As a result of his newfound knowledge, he decided that each day he would take the biggest fare of the day and deposit it into an investment account. After years of continuing this daily ritual, he ended up purchasing the entire taxicab company.

Statistics show:

- 58% of adults NEVER READ another book for the REST of their lives
- 42% of college graduates NEVER READ another book after college graduation
- 80% of US Families did not buy or read a book last year
- 70% of US adults have not been in a bookstore in the last five years[55]

What are the rituals that will take you to your dream?

Jesus is our greatest example, and in the book of Luke we read about Jesus as a young boy of eight years old. Notice that we hear nothing more until he is twelve years old. The only point made in reference to the life of Jesus is, "the child grew." One translation says, "And Jesus matured, growing up in both body and spirit."

You should be on a quest for continual growth. I want to challenge you to do something to continually educate yourself by reading for twenty minutes each day. It's a great place to start if you are like me and you don't enjoy reading. I used to loathe the thought of sitting down quietly and just reading. That was so boring to me. However, I began setting the timer on my phone to read for twenty minutes, and I recognized that the more I practiced this habit, the more I began to desire it. Why? My thinking was changing.

Clement Stone (publisher of *Success* magazine, worth $800 million) had an interview with young Jack Canfield. He said, "First, I have a question for you. Do you watch television?"

Jack said, "Yes."

Stone asked, "How many hours a day do you watch?"

Jack said, "I don't know. I watch *Good Morning, America,* the local news, *The Tonight Show.* Probably around three hours a day."

Stone said, "Cut out one hour a day."

Jack said, "Ok. But why?"

Stone said, "If you cut out that one hour a day and you multiply that by 365 days, that gives you 365 extra hours. Divide 365 hours by a 40 hour work week and you'll have nine and a half weeks of productive time." Then, Stone said, "I want that time."

Jack inquired, "What do you want me to do?"

Stone said, "I want you to READ! Read in your field that will help you. Read stories. Read psychology. Read management. Read media. Read about this arena that we play the game in. If you do this, you will not only become more valuable to me, but to yourself."

Jack Canfield later became recognized in the *Guinness*

Book of World Records for having seven books on the *New York Times* bestseller list simultaneously. Do you realize that if you were to read one book each week that would be fifty-two books in a year? In ten years' time that is 520 books! Jack Canfield says, "That would make you in the top 1% in your field."[56]

Have you ever been bitten by an elephant? How about a mosquito? These may sound like silly questions, but the point is that it's the little things that bite you! It's the small, seemingly insignificant, habits that you neglect that distract you from your dreams.

Think about the little excuses we give ourselves:

- "It's just one day."
- "What does it matter?"
- "Nobody even sees what I'm doing?"
- "Reading for twenty minutes is not going to make a difference."
- "I have so far to go; it's not even worth it."

I can't hire someone to listen to messages, read books, declare my goals out loud, express gratitude to God for what He's done in my life . . . for me. I think motivational speaker, Tony Robbins, explained the by-product of these disciplines best when he said, "People are rewarded in public for what they practice in private." You will be rewarded for your routine.

Larry Bird, one of the greatest professional basketball players, wasn't known for being the most athletically talented player. Despite his limitations in certain skills, he led the Boston Celtics to three world championships and became one of the best NBA players of all time. How? His routine.

Growing up, his morning routine was to practice 500 free throw shots every morning before school. Yes, every single morning. His routine paid off! He was one of the most consistent free throw shooters in the history of the NBA.[57]

Years ago, my dad and I were at Dallas/Fort Worth International Airport on our way to a conference when he wanted to stop by Starbucks and grab a cup of coffee. He ordered a low fat, no caffeine cup of coffee with 2% milk and no whipped cream. The barista yelled, "One medium why bother!" Dad said, "What did you call it?" She said, "A cup of why bother!" In other words, what's the point in getting any coffee at all when you're leaving out all the good stuff!

We tend to feel the same way when we launch our new success routine. Why bother listening to a message on my way to work? Why bother cutting out one hour of television each night to learn? Why bother declaring my dreams out loud? Why bother expressing gratitude when I don't have much to be grateful for? Why even bother making a pointless vision board?

In the beginning, all of your efforts will feel so insignificant, and you have miles to go, so why bother? The most successful people in the world bother! Every day matters. Every inch of progress is still progress. In 2002, when I began these little habits of personal development, I never dreamed I would still be practicing them. In addition, I never imagined what a monumental change they would produce in my life and ultimately, enable me to live my dreams.

What is simple to do is also simple not to do. The biggest difference in dreamers and dream-achievers is that those who achieve their aspirations are willing to do what others are not willing to do. I can't help but think how most people don't see me Monday morning at 5:00 a.m., rolling out of bed, slipping on my jogging clothes, going outside in the dark to jump in my car, driving to the gym, lifting weights, and walking on the treadmill, while listening to messages for a full hour. They don't see me return home, go into my home office, sit on my chaise lounge, spend time in prayer over my vision board, write down what I am most grateful for, express praise to God, declare my dreams out loud, rejoice as if they're done, then shower, get dressed, and go to work.

Most people scroll through our Instagram or Facebook page and just think, "Wow! She does book signings in Paris, France! She's on television. She just launched another new book. She speaks to thousands of people." My response to that is always, the secret of your future is hidden in your daily routine. Change your routine and you can change your life.

Habit #3 - Focus On Three Priorities

Focus is the key word in this chapter. If you want to come to the end of this year with GREAT RESULTS, then you must be highly focused. Focus is the opposite of DISTRACTIONS. When we have too many priorities, we lose our focus and end up accomplishing nothing.

I know that I have challenged you to write down 101 dreams that you want to accomplish in your lifetime. I have also instructed you on how to identify and list your top ten goals for the year (or the next 12-18 months). Although it may seem contradictory to my previous advice, I want you to narrow your focus even more.

Warren Buffet has a method that has helped him achieve his unprecedented success. Here is what he recommends to realize your most prominent goals:

- Write out all of your priorities.
- Narrow the list down to your top three.
- Throw away the rest of the list.

Contrary to the total Buffet method, I do not recommend you throw away the rest of your list; however, I am advising that you get laser-focused on your top three most important goals at this time. In other words, if you achieved these three goals, you would be exhilarated.

When Warren Buffet was asked to boil the keys to his success down to one single principle, this was his shocking response, "For every 100 great opportunities that are brought to me, I say no 99 times!" He attributes his success to his ability to say no—in other words, his ability to stay focused.

Darren Hardy asked the late Steve Jobs what he was most proud of in terms of all the breakthrough products he and Apple built. Perhaps you'll be as surprised at his response as I was. Jobs replied, "I am as proud of what we don't do as I am of what we do!" He went on to say, "Deciding what *not to do* is as important as deciding what *to do*."[58]

> IF YOU HAVE MORE THAN THREE PRIORITIES, YOU DON'T HAVE ANY.
> —JIM COLLINS

This statement bears true for companies, entrepreneurs, stay-at-home moms, authors, pastors, teachers, real estate agents, etc. Focus is just as much about saying no as it is saying yes. What will you start saying no to in order to achieve your most important goals this year?

Actor Will Smith said, "To have the level of success that I want to have, it's difficult to spread it out and do multiple things. It takes such a desperate, obsessive focus. You've really got to focus with all of your fiber and all of your heart and all of your creativity."[59]

What Are Your Three Strategic Priorities?

Darren Hardy tells the most intense story of focus involving Sir Richard Branson in his teaching called "Darren Hardy Shares Secrets of Great Achievers." Hardy shared how he was approached by a friend who inquired as to how he could arrange for Richard Branson to speak at his success conference since Darren had a relationship with Branson. The friend went on to make this commitment, "We will pay him one hundred thousand dollars to speak at our conference for one hour."

Darren agreed to ask. He reached out to Branson's office, and they declined the offer. Darren reported the negative response to his friend who then said, "Well, tell him we'll pay him $250,000 for an hour!" They called back. Branson declined again.

Determined now to see what it would take to have this gentleman who runs 300 companies worth $4 billion come and speak, he increased his generous offer: "We will send a private jet to pick him up and take him to the conference. As soon as his foot hits the pavement, we will have him back in the plane in under an hour, and we will pay $500,000!" Branson was not interested.

Dumbfounded, they said, "Okay. Just give us a number! Whatever it takes, give us a number!" Branson's office responded with this amazing answer: "Richard is focused on three strategic priorities right now and he will only allow us to allocate his calendar to something that significantly contributes to the achievement of one of those three strategic priorities. And speaking for a fee at any price is not one of them."

Darren Hardy points out this billion-dollar remark from this story, "Keep in mind: Richard Branson didn't just arrive at this focus. It was this focus all along the way that he ended up with 300 companies worth $4 billion!"[60]

Obviously, we cannot walk around saying no to everything and achieve success, but we do need to narrow our focus by recognizing the distractions that are pulling on us. You may have heard the phrase that it's better to be world class at a few things than mediocre at most things.

What can you focus on that will help you become world class at the dream you're most passionate about? There are some skills we need to learn and make them part of our top three priorities because improvement in a particular one will dramatically affect, or have a ripple effect on, the achievement of the other dreams and goals.

For example, what if your goals included:

- Eliminate credit card debt of $15,000.
- Enjoy a Bahamas vacation with my family for $7,000.
- Pay off my car of $8,000.
- Save $5,000.
- Obtain my Realtor's license.
- Attend two success conferences.
- Read twelve books by December 31st.

Notice, out of these seven important goals for the year, there are three that could be identified as priorities and if achieved, would ultimately affect the rest of the goals. If this goal-setting individual were to (1) attend two success conferences, (2) read twelve books, (3) obtain Realtor's license then the effects of these goals achieved could potentially increase their personal revenue. An increase in personal revenue would afford him/her the means to eliminate credit card debt, enjoy a dream vacation, pay the balance on a car note, and save money for the future.

What do you need to identify as your top three priorities that could drastically impact the rest of your goals? Is it becoming a better writer? Is it learning a foreign language? If you were bi-lingual, could it potentially double your income and help you achieve your financial goals? If so, then that would be one of your top priorities for the year.

Is it developing better communication skills? Is it playing the guitar? Is it writing songs? Is it taking a class? Is it finishing a manuscript?

Habit #4 - Focus On One Goal at a Time

Dave Ramsey says, "Total, sold-out, focused intensity is required to win. You can't get ready, fire and then aim with money, and you can't try to do six things at the same time." Ramsey goes so far to instruct people to stop doing anything with money except paying the minimum payments. Stop 401K contributions (temporarily), stop saving (temporarily), stop paying an extra $3 on debts, and to totally focus paying off the smallest debt at a time! And then move on to the next.[61]

For example, if you have written down three big financial goals, then in order to achieve any of them, you must get focused on one at a time until it is accomplished.

Maybe if you listed financial goals such as:

- Save $10,000 by December 31st.
- Eliminate credit card debt of $7,000 by December 31st.

- Pay off school loans of $3,000 by September 1st.

If so, focus on one at a time. Which one do you allocate your time, energy, and resources to? The smallest one. You focus on eliminating the smallest debt first. Your major goal should be paying off the school loan of $3,000. Focus all extra income toward achieving that one goal. Do not even consider saving money at this point. Pay off the school loan and then work diligently toward the second goal of debt reduction. Then, start saving money.

Years ago, I had my top ten goals for the year, which included three different books on my heart to write. I was equally passionate about each topic, and I knew the Lord wanted me to publish these works. However, because I wasn't focused on one project at a time, I was consumed with stress, frustration, and anxiety because none of them were complete. I had three half-written books impacting no one.

Finally, I had to eliminate the distraction of the other two books and focus on one single manuscript until it was completed. Once I finished it, sent it off to the publisher, then I could move my focus onto the next manuscript. As John Maxwell puts it, "Too many priorities paralyze us."

Darren Hardy explains why animal trainers carry a four-legged stool when they enter a cage of lions. If you've ever observed this at the circus, you'll remember lion tamers carry whips, a pistol, and that rinky-dink wooden stool. Hardy claims that the

> THE ONLY WAY TO GET AHEAD IS TO GET BETTER. IF YOU'RE NOT CONTINUALLY IMPROVING IN THE MOST IMPORTANT AREAS, THEN YOU'RE NOT MOVING AHEAD.
> —DARREN HARDY

little stool is the most important tool of the trainer. Notice how the lion tamer holds the stool by the back and aims the four legs toward the face of the untamed animal. Why in the world does he do that? How can a lightweight piece of furniture protect a human being from a ferocious lion? Simply put, the animal tries to focus on all four legs at once. In an effort to look at too many things at the same time, a certain paralysis overtakes him, and the lion becomes docile, weak, and disabled. Clearly, his attention is fragmented and he becomes ill-equipped for what he was designed to be and do.[62]

The same is true for you and me when we lose our focus. We become paralyzed with inefficiency. Satan wants you tame, weak, and disabled so you'll never achieve God's plan for your life! So, he overwhelms you with too many priorities.

We have to remember that there will always be an unlimited list of goals we need to accomplish, and "priorities" are always fighting for our attention; but, if

> THE MAN WHO CHASES
> TWO RABBITS,
> CATCHES NEITHER.
> —CONFUCIOUS

we really want to reach our goals, we must learn the skill of saying no. We must avoid those distractions competing for our attention to pull us away from our top priorities.

When Joel Osteen took over the position as the Lead Pastor for Lakewood Church (the largest church in America), he was trying to do everything. A former television editor now pastor over thousands of people, he had so many responsibilities. He was trying to do it all. His pastoral duties included everything from preaching and weddings to baptisms and funerals while also maintaining his previous role of editing commercials, adjusting lights on stage, etc. However, with Joel being spread out all over the place, the organization came to a standstill. Progress was stagnant. Joel realized he had to stand back and determine the one thing that contributes the most to the success of his organization. He figured out that it was that 22 minutes on Sunday![63]

His inspiring, faith-filled message of hope was the most important contribution he could make to impact the overall success of the church. When he came to this realization, he stopped doing everything else and focused on that 22-minute message.

If that weekly message was inspiring, hopeful, excellent then it drove the entire organization. Every other department grew and impacted more lives as a result of his focus. What is it for you? Which area do you need to get laser-focused because it will impact other areas of your life?

- Is it learning a foreign language?
- Is it better communication skills?
- Is it writing?
- Is it delivering better messages?
- Is it playing guitar?
- Is it writing songs?
- Is it marketing?
- Is it selling?
- Is it taking a class to obtain a special license?

Remember, what you achieve isn't nearly as important as who you become while you're working toward the goals on your vision board. As you're working on the goals, the goals are working on you. Look at your calendar and schedule time to adapt these new behaviors of listening and reading into your routine.

If you want to accumulate more on the outside, become

more on the inside. Ask yourself, *Who do I need to become to achieve my dreams?*

God Can't Use You Publicly Until . . .

You've gotten victory privately! God sees everything. During all of those mornings when you force yourself to get up early and pray while everyone else sleeps in, you're becoming more. For each lunch break when you read an encouraging devotional instead of wasting the entire break scanning through social media, you're becoming more. In every commute spent listening to a podcast, you're becoming more. Preparation time is never wasted time.

It's been said that the wealthiest places on earth are cemeteries. In the graveyards, there are books that were never written, songs that were never sung and businesses that were never started. Don't go to the grave with your dreams still in you. Determine today that you will gain and maintain good habits that others will admire, that God will promote, and that will lead you to prosperity and success.

> SUCCESS IS THE SUM OF SMALL EFFORTS REPEATED DAY IN AND DAY OUT.
> —ROBERT COLLIER

In closing this chapter, I want you to hear the advice of a very wealthy, very successful 100 year old man who was featured in *Success* magazine. When asked what he considered to be the most important habit for becoming a success, he handed them a single sheet of paper and said, "That's it! Every single word on there is vital, but that's it!" The paper read:"Do fewer things more often! And get better at them!"[64]

If you want to succeed, focus is your key.

ACTION STEP

Think about the most important things in your life. What do you need to focus on improving that would make the greatest difference towards you achieving your dreams?

TEN
THE HIDDEN KEY TO LIVING YOUR DREAMS
What Gets God's Attention

> DO NOT BE DECEIVED; GOD CANNOT BE
> MOCKED: A MAN REAPS WHAT HE SOWS.
> —GALATIANS 6:7

How will you ever attain the money needed to accomplish your big dreams? Will the finances ever be enough to achieve your highest expectations? Why is it that some people seem to prosper financially more than others? The people who succeed at reaching their highest dreams are those who have tapped into this hidden key known as the power of giving.

My dad taught me this profound principle that states: You may not have what you need, but you're never without the seed that will produce it. Basically, whenever you have a need, sow a seed.

In comparison to a farmer who looks out at his empty fields, he knows that complaints over his lack will not produce his dream crops, but seed will. If that farmer chooses to hold on to his seed, that's all he will ever have.

If he chooses to sow it, the crops will multiply. We always reap more than we sow!

Many people who have a dream, especially a financial dream, think it's best to hold tight to what they have; but, in reality, it is wise to release it. When you give your finances to the Kingdom of God, you are opening the door for God to give you back more.

> *"It is possible to give and yet become richer."*
> *—Proverbs 11:24*

God's system of finances never fails. Your giving produces miracles. Your giving positions you to receive more in your life. Your giving represents your faith in your future. Bottom line: when you get involved in building God's dream, He will get involved in building yours.

What are you sowing for? Galatians 6:7 says, "Do not be deceived; God cannot be mocked: A man reaps what he sows." Literally, what you give is what you get.

If you know exactly what you're giving for, you'll recognize the harvest when it comes. For example, when a farmer plants his seed, he doesn't just toss it out across the ground and then wonder what he will produce. How foolish would that be? He knows exactly what he desires; therefore, he sows what he wants. If you sow tomato seeds, you wouldn't expect corn. And, if you sow apples, you should expect a harvest of apples.

There are natural consequences to our acts of giving. If you sow clothes, you'll reap more clothes. If you sow jewelry, you'll reap jewelry. If you sow money, you'll reap money. We reap in kind to what we sow. The bottom line: if money is needed, then money needs to be sown.

Years ago, I desperately wanted some new clothes. Like

most women, I had a vision for a new wardrobe! I didn't have the extra finances at the time to go out and purchase anything I wanted, so I simply practiced what I am teaching you. You may not have what you need, but you are never without the seed that will produce it.

I went through my closet and collected five large bags full of clothing to give away. I was operating under the principle of "sow much, reap much." Plus, I didn't just throw a bunch of t-shirts in a bag and call it "seed." I selected beautiful dresses, tops, skirts, and even a few amazing pairs of stilettos! I prayed about who to bless, and then I cheerfully gave it away knowing, with confidence, that I would reap what I sowed.

Within one month, a friend gave me a $350 gift card to my favorite clothing store! It also happened to be my birthday month and, for some reason, my friends and family kept giving me gift cards to department stores and cash to "Go shopping," they said. Sow clothes, reap clothes. It's the law of sowing and reaping.

In comparison to your vision board where you have images of what you desire in your future, a farmer has a visual representation of his harvest on the package of seeds. That depicts his vision. However, that farmer realizes that only looking at the package of seeds will not profit him. Simply speaking to the package will not benefit him. Expressing gratitude for the seeds alone will not produce results. He must sow the seeds.

Your dreams are no different. You must sow for each of your dreams if you want a harvest in your life. I am convinced that this is the hidden key to living your dreams!

I want to point out that I do not think you need to give a car away (unless God instructs you to do that) in order to receive the car that's displayed on your vision board. I have known many people to do that, but many people cannot afford to release their only form of transportation. I do believe you need to give what you can financially and name that offering as "money for my car." This is what Jesse Duplantis calls, "Naming Your Seed." If you don't name your seed, you won't recognize the harvest when it comes.

In fact, in the *Dream It. Pin It. Live It. Workbook,* I have a section for you to list your donations and for naming your seed sown for the dreams you believe to harvest in your life. I have been doing this for years, and it always amazes me to see the harvest manifested next to the seed sown!

*"A man's harvest in life will
depend entirely on what he sows."
– Galatians 6:7 [J.B. Phillips New Testament]*

In my book, *Imagine Big,* I shared the story of how my husband, Rodney, and I were getting ready to build our second home. At the same time, I was four months pregnant and eager to move into a bigger house. We had one snag. In order to reduce the monthly payment to an amount we could afford at that time, we would be required to put $48,000 down as our initial down payment!

I remember vividly as we both sat there in the builder's office, swallowed real hard and said, "Okay, we will have the $48,000 by the deadline."

You have to know where we were financially at that time in order to comprehend what a gutsy declaration that was. We were living paycheck to paycheck; our salaries were around $40,000 each, and we had a mere $1,000 in our savings account! It was August of 1996 and we were scheduled to move in by January 30, 1997! How in the world could we come up with $48,000 in five months!

Rodney and I went home from that surreal moment and

took a hard look at our finances. After we recognized that all we had was $1,000 to put toward the down payment, we also remembered this principle, "You may not have what you need, but you are never without the seed that will produce it."

Rodney and I both agreed that what we had ($1,000) wasn't enough to meet our need ($48,000) so it became our significant seed. We gave all of it away! We gave money because we desperately needed money. Now, $1,000 may not seem like much to you, but to us, it was very significant because it was all we had.

After we sowed the best we had, we took a picture of the blueprints of our dream home and taped it to the refrigerator door in our kitchen. I kept a copy of it on my desk at work as well. Beneath the picture I wrote, "Thank You, Jesus, for $48,000 by January 30, 1997." And I listed increments of the thousands needed this way:

$48,000	$38,000	$28,000	$18,000	$8,000
$47,000	$37,000	$27,000	$17,000	$7,000
$46,000	$36,000	$26,000	$16,000	$6,000
$45,000	$35,000	$25,000	$15,000	$5,000
$44,000	$34,000	$24,000	$14,000	$4,000
$43,000	$33,000	$23,000	$13,000	$3,000
$42,000	$32,000	$22,000	$12,000	$2,000
$41,000	$31,000	$21,000	$11,000	$1,000
$40,000	$30,000	$20,000	$10,000	PAID IN FULL!!!!
$39,000	$29,000	$19,000	$ 9,000	

We kept that vision before our eyes daily. We declared our dreams out loud. We expressed gratitude for the opportunities we believed were coming our way to increase our income. We didn't know *how* it would happen; we just had confidence that it *would* happen. We were applying the law of seedtime and harvest.

Remember, it is not your job to figure out how your dreams will manifest. Your responsibility is to stay focused on the vision, sow seed toward it and trust God. Remember this phrase: When what you see inside becomes more real than what you see outside, it's just a matter of time. God will bring ideas, opportunities, resources, and relationships to make your dream happen!

And that's exactly what happened. God began bringing my husband and I both opportunities like never before to make money! We did everything from selling pinball machines found at a garage sale to ghostwriting books for other authors. Rodney went door-to-door painting address numbers on the curbs outside people's homes. I taught French to children after school. We seized every opportunity we could find to make money . . . and God continued to bring them.

We rejoiced every time we were able to mark another one thousand dollars off the vision paper! And yes, it looked quite scary when we still lacked $20,000 to reach our goal with only six weeks to go! But God is faithful! As we proactively looked for opportunities to work, to make extra money and to diligently pursue this vision with intense desire, the day came when we were scheduled to meet with the bank to prove that we had the amount needed for closing.

We had earned $38,600 in five short months! However, the amount needed was $48,000. As we sat in the bank sweating a little bit, the loan officer came back to us and said, "After reviewing everything, it appears that your home has come in under budget and the down payment needed is $38,000 to move in!" We had more than enough!

I can't help but wonder how long it would have taken us to achieve that goal if we had held on to our seed instead of giving it. I have experienced this time and time again in my personal life and in my organization. I have received countless testimonies from others who have reaped the benefits of giving, and you will, too.

Give to Someone Else's Dream

When you invest your money into someone else's dream, you actually help yourself more than you help them. You strategically put yourself in a position to receive from God!

> IT IS ONE OF THE BEAUTIFUL COMPENSATIONS OF THIS LIFE THAT NO MAN CAN SINCERELY TRY TO HELP ANOTHER WITHOUT HELPING HIMSELF.
> —RALPH WALDO EMERSON

Here is a testimony from a precious lady who had great needs of her own, but gave to our ministry outreach (helping troubled teenage girls) and look what her giving produced:

> I thank you from the bottom of my heart for the opportunity to give into your ministry. I put into practice what I was learning from you, and you helped me bring to the forefront some dreams that were slowly simmering. In January, I committed to planting my "debt-free seed" into your ministry. I determined that your ministry was good soil that would

also give me a hundred-fold return. I am standing on Mark 10:30, "But he shall receive a hundredfold now in this time . . . "

I had a lot of debt because of school loans. To be exact, it was $193,550! I know, bad. So I started with a very small seed, like that of the mustard seed. LOL. I committed to double my seed each month. And I mean, like never before, I put aside money every chance I got because I knew that as I got closer to the end of the year, to my December 31st deadline, that my seed would be much bigger. I have never taken on this big a commitment in finances before.

I sent you 52 cents for January and then $1.04 for February in one envelope. I sent it in change and had to tape it so it wouldn't fall out. In March, it was $2.08. Each month I doubled it. We called our offering "Sell of Property" as we had two pieces we were selling.

Well, one sold and we closed on it October 1st!

I told my husband, "Let's go ahead and use some of the money from the sell of the property to get the rest of this seed in the ground." This letter has our seed for October: $266.24 and November: $532.48 and December: $1,064.96! Combined total of $1,863.68!

Isn't it awesome how a mere 52 cents and a pledge to double it each month can grow to this amount? Once again, thank you so much and watch for my next letter.

You Can't Out Give God

You are the most like God when you give! The most famous verse in the Bible, John 3:16, says, "For God so loved ... that He gave." When we love, we give! The desire you have to help others is something God put in you and when you obey that prompting, you actually help yourself.

God never forgets a seed sown. Never! I heard one minister say, "Your seed may leave your hands, but it will never leave your life." When you give tithes and offerings to God, it is one of the best guarantees of prosperity ever known!

Interestingly, my organization has never been more blessed than we are right now. At the same time, we have never given as much as we have given recently. We have purposely looked for areas to give and give big! God honors a giving heart.

Invest in the dreams you pasted on your vision board. How? Give a financial gift. Years ago, I had a big vision for five major areas of my new organization. I couldn't conceive how these huge goals could come to pass. I did not have the resources, the connections, or the capability to make them happen. So, I wrote my vision clearly, printed images for each dream, began speaking positive declarations over each one, expressed gratitude for their fulfillment, and then I sowed a financial seed for each and every one.

For example:

- *TV* – I had a desire to have a successful Christian broadcast. I was very clear and specific about what I was wanted in terms of viewer response to the broadcast. I gave the best financial offering I could into a ministry that already had a successful broadcast. Once we launched our broadcast, our response surpassed my highest expectations!

- *Books* – When I had a dream to write my own books, I gave a significant financial gift to a successful author whose books impacted my life. Nine months later, I walked into a Barnes and Noble bookstore and saw my books on the shelf.

- *France* – When God first began to speak to me about making a difference in the nation of France, my first move was to give a financial gift to pastors of a church in Paris. My books are now in French and sold in the largest bookstores in Paris!

- *Women's Conference* – I had a desire to launch a conference for women and teenage girls long before anyone wanted to hear a word I had to say. I printed a photo of myself superimposed on a stage speaking to thousands of people. I began speaking to that vision. Then, I gave a financial gift to my mentor, Joyce Meyer, who hosts women's conferences across the globe. Today, I host the ICING Women's Conference in convention centers.

- *Helping Troubled Teens* – I knew I wanted to help teenage girls who were pregnant, inflicting self-harm, suffering from eating disorders, and being rescued from human trafficking, but I didn't know how to start. So, I gave the best financial gift I had into Mercy Ministries (an organization committed to helping and housing troubled teenage girls). As a result, I am now able to provide the teaching resources for girls in homes all across the United States.

The kind of future you have depends entirely on the kind

of seeds you sow right now. How many times have you given an offering or made a charitable donation without thinking about what you were sowing that seed for? Decide exactly what you need, and then turn it into a seed.

Give More to Receive More

We receive in life proportionately to what we give. It really is a simple principle: the more you give, the more you receive. The Bible clearly points out that those who give generously will be blessed more than those who give grudgingly or out of necessity. "Remember this: whoever sows sparingly will also reap sparingly, and whoever sows generously will also reap generously. Each of you should give what you have decided in your heart to give, not reluctantly or under compulsion, for God loves a cheerful giver." (2 Corinthians 9:6-7 NIV)

Never give under pressure. God is more interested in your heart than the amount of money you're giving. Seed . . . time . . . and harvest!

Nothing good grows overnight. It is a process. All farmers know the practice of patience. When God instructs us to give, he suggests that it will require a length of time. Scripture even says, "God will bring forth fruit in His time." (1 Corinthians 3:6) Notice it is not in "our time." We all want that harvest in our lives, but often we want it ahead of God's timing.

The Law of Seedtime and Harvest reveals to us that we don't go from seed to harvest without time in the middle. We want instant results or else we declare that it isn't working. Be wise like a farmer knowing that harvest takes a little time.

We know from the Word of God that there is a season

for everything. (See Ecclesiastes 3:1) This lets us know that we don't live in the same seasons all the time. Never allow yourself to get jealous over someone else who could be in the "harvest season" while you are still in the "planting season." Just remember that they also had to plant and wait. Let their results encourage you with confidence that you are next in line.

Although it can be frustrating when you're waiting, don't start questioning God or trying to figure out how to help Him. Put your complete trust in His timing, and it will eliminate aggravation and worry. God will cause your harvest to arrive right on time. Things may appear not to be changing, but nothing can stop the Law of Seedtime and Harvest from working in your life. Just because your dream has been delayed does not mean it's been denied.

When God put it on my heart to resign my position as CEO for an organization where I had been employed for twenty-two years to open my own headquarters over an hour away in Rockwall, Texas, this decision involved selling my house. Not only did I need to relocate my home, but my staff members moving with me would need to sell their houses and relocate as well.

Consistently, I practice this principle of sowing toward my dreams. I needed my house to sell, they needed their houses to sell, so I gave (sowed) a large financial gift to each employee and declared that this was "seed" for all of our houses to sell.

Immediately, their houses sold! I mean, one-by-one they were updating me with victory reports of how fast they closed on their homes. One gentleman put the sign in his yard and that very night a buyer knocked on the door saying, "I want your house!"

Yet, I waited and waited and waited for seven, long, painful, trying, frustrating months! I had to enroll my daughter in her new school in the new city with no house to live in. We had to live in a hotel for three of the seven months! Time was going by. Expenses were increasing. Tears were shed each night as my daughter returned "home" to the little hotel room our family shared together.

We continued to trust God that His timing is always right even though it may not make sense to our minds. Seven months after we sowed our best financial gifts into our staff, we received a phone call from our realtor saying, "You didn't just receive one offer on your house, you received two offers in one day!"

We went seven months with no offers, and in one single moment, two potential buyers got into a bidding war over our house increasing the sale of our property by $30,000! God's timing is always better than our deadline.

If your dream seems delayed, wait for it. Do not give up. This is why God says, "Do not grow weary in well doing, for in due season, you will reap if you faint not."

ACTION STEP

I want to challenge you to put a demand on your faith in God by giving a financial gift or sowing a seed of some kind for each and every one or your dreams. It could be one large donation for all of your dreams or individual gifts for each dream. There is no right or wrong way to invest in your dreams.

Let God speak to you about what to give and where to give it. Listen to His instruction for your finances. Hearing his voice is the best assurance of receiving the harvest He desires for you to have. The point is, if you're down to your last dollar, don't hold on to it, sow it. Plant that financial seed in the ground and watch God multiply it.

ELEVEN
IDEAS TO GET YOUR CREATIVITY FLOWING
Places to Go, Things to See, Aspirations to Achieve

INSPIRATION EXISTS, BUT IT HAS
TO FIND US WORKING.
—PABLO PICASSO

It doesn't matter how big or small your list of goals, plans, and activities is. The focus is on your zest for living life to the fullest and fulfilling every dream God has put in your heart to do. Plan the highlights of your life. Live on purpose. Remove limitations. Maximize your moments. Below I have provided suggested lists you can create to plan your goals and dreams along with examples of how I would fill them in. They will be included in the workbook with space for you to fill in your own or you can use your own journal for this.

#1. List countries you would like to visit.

- France
- Spain
- Italy

- England
- Australia
- USA
- Brazil
- Japan
- New Zealand

#2. List things you would like to collect.

- Postcards
- Stamps
- Keychains
- Snow globes
- Coins
- Baseball cards
- Sea shells
- Rocks

#3. List activities you would like to try.

- Surfing
- Parasailing
- Snow skiing
- Horseback riding

#4. List beaches you would like to visit (and collect sand).

- Waikiki Beach (Honolulu, Hawaii)
- Muscle Beach
- Surfer's Paradise (Gold Coast, Australia)
- Negril, Jamaica
- South Beach, Miami

- Copacabana Beach, Rio de Janeiro
- Cape Cod, Massachusetts

#5. List monuments you would like to see.
- Mount Rushmore
- Taj Mahal
- The Egyptian Pyramids
- The Great Wall of China

#6. List books you would like to read.

- *The Bible*
- *Think and Grow Rich* by Napoleon Hill
- *If Satan Can't Steal Your Joy, He Can't Keep Your Goods* by Jerry Savelle
- *Developing the Leader Within You* by John Maxwell
- *The Seven Habits of Highly Effective People* by Steven Covey

#7. List plays you would like to see.

- *Les Miserables*
- *The Lion King*
- *Phantom of the Opera*
- *Jersey Boys*
- *Mama Mia!*

#8. List classes you would like to take.

- Cooking
- Cake decorating

- Scrapbooking
- Marketing

#9. List museums you would like to visit.

- Le Louvre (Paris, France)
- The Smithsonian Institute (Washington D.C.)
- The British Museum (London, England)
- The Metropolitan Museum of Art (New York City, New York)

#10. List parades you would like to view.

- Macy's Thanksgiving Day Parade (New York City)
- The Rose Parade (Pasadena, California)
- Mardi Gras (New Orleans, Louisiana)
- St. Patrick's Day Parade (Boston, Massachusetts)
- Inaugural Parade (Washington, D.C.)

#11. List a language(s) you would like to learn.

- French
- English
- German
- Spanish
- Italian
- Japanese
- Dutch

#12. List states you would like to visit.

- Texas
- California
- Florida
- New York
- North Carolina
- South Carolina
- Massachusetts
- Louisiana
- All 50

#13. List special events you would like to witness.

- Summer Olympic Games
- New Year's Eve in Times Square
- Super Bowl Game
- The World Series
- Championship Boxing Match

#14. List celebrities you would like to meet.

- Jim Carrey
- Oprah Winfrey
- Denzel Washington
- Reese Witherspoon
- Sandra Bullock
- Matthew McConnaughey
- Julia Roberts

#15. List organizations you would like to support.

- Ministries
- Local church
- Girls' home
- Organization for orphans
- Women's shelters
- Homeless shelters
- Disaster relief funds

#16. List creative dates you would like to have.

- Go on a romantic picnic
- Ride a gondola in Venice, Italy
- Ride in a horse and carriage
- Spend the day at a spa resort

#17. List adventures you'd like to experience.

- Run a marathon
- Go scuba diving
- Feed dolphins
- Climb a mountain
- Fly in a hot-air balloon
- Drive a race car around the track

#18. List creative projects you'd like to try.

- Write an autobiography
- Host a theme party
- Join a book club

- Write a song
- Get a college degree
- Publish an article in my local newspaper
- Create a scrapbook of your life

#19. List personal or family growth opportunities you'd like to explore.

- Adopt a child
- Build my dream home
- Have a summer home
- Learn CPR
- Sponsor a child

#20. List charitable or volunteer activities you'd like to participate in.

- Take Christmas gifts to a nursing home
- Volunteer at a children's hospital
- Go on a mission trip
- Volunteer at church
- Mentor a teenager
- Send flowers to an elderly person

TWELVE
VISION BOARD SUCCESS STORIES
Be Inspired by Others Who Dared to Dream

FIND YOUR VOICE AND INSPIRE OTHERS TO FIND THEIRS.
—STEPHEN COVEY

In this chapter, I am sharing testimonials sent to me by people who followed the principles I've laid out in this book and have seen them in action in their lives. I hope you will be inspired by their stories and create a vision board to realize your own dreams.

Permission to Dream – A Vision for a Horse Farm

When my husband and I started our business many years ago, we were both car wash employees with a very small income. We were just trying to survive and it was really hard for me to dream. Our mentors told us to put our dreams and goals before our eyes. We did not have a vision board, but we used our refrigerator as our vision board. I remember sitting down and really thinking for the first time about what I really wanted. I had always wanted a nice horse from the time I was a little girl. I really didn't think this could happen. I was an adult now and needed to think about responsible things. But they said "anything." I cut out a picture of 11 horses standing at a fence in a beautiful pasture. I remember a brown horse, white horse, a spotted horse and several other colors, shapes and sizes. Feeling very silly, I taped the picture to the fridge. I put this picture up even though I only wanted one horse, but couldn't decide which one. It stayed on the refrigerator for years, It was torn and stained. When we moved out of that tiny house, I took the picture with me to our new home and put it back on the refrigerator. Today, we have a 34 acre horse farm with 11 horses, 2 miniature donkeys and a pony. I also have two beautiful show horses at a training facility. If you look out into the beautiful rolling pastures of our farm, you will see horses that look almost exactly like the ones in the picture on the refrigerator from years ago. It is a beautiful reminder to me that the Lord loves us so much. He wants us to have the desires of our heart. He has blessed me far above what I could have imagined. It is more than the horses. It is proof that all things are possible to those that continue to believe and never give up.

Pam – North Carolina

Clarity Is Key – A Vision for TV Equipment

As a church, God had given us a four step plan for our vision: Cover the city, bless our neighbors, send to the nations, and touch the world.

Our role as the technical team was to fulfill this vision and accommodate the mandate that God had for the church through media.

The first thing we did in order to fulfill this big vision that God had for us was to write down and itemize the things we needed to make it possible without looking at cost. This was inspired by Terri Savelle's first visit to minister in Bristol, England a few years ago when she taught us the importance of writing down the vision and having a dream board.

Here's what we placed on our dream board:

The TV station equipment

Radio station equipment

The layout of how we wanted the TV and Radio station to look like.

We kept our eyes open and over the coming months we kept coming across each item that we needed. We were able to obtain all the items written and all for a fraction of the standard cost.

Carmel Church – Bristol, UK

The 30-Day Challenge – A Vision for a Mission Trip and New Job

Terri, I heard you speak at my church a few weeks ago. There were two things I was believing for. #1 For my visa to allow me to go on a missions trip to India. I made a copy of my passport and wrote the word visa across it. I hung it on my mirror with a picture of the children I'll be ministering to. I laid my hand on it and spoke over it first thing every morning and every night before I went to bed. Even though some missionaries were being denied, I never doubted I would get mine. I got my visa on Wednesday and I will be leaving tomorrow from Raleigh to go to India! #2 I wanted a new job with better hours to free me up to do more of what God wants me to do. I had an interview last Wednesday. That evening I wrote down that I got the job and put it on my mirror. I prayed and spoke over it. The very next afternoon they called me and offered me the job! Thank you so much for your wisdom and God bless you.

Mary M. – North Carolina

What Goes on Your Board - A Vision for a Kidney

Hi Terri, I want to share a testimony with you. You inspired me to start "The Dream Party" ministry and not only has my life changed, but many other lives are being changed also. Since it was established we have had some great testimonies. But I believe the most powerful one is the most recent one about my nephew, Andre. Andre had been waiting for a new kidney for over 10 years, because both his kidneys failed. Andre's mom created her dream journal and put a picture of Andre with a picture of a new kidney that someone had drawn for her in her journal. She also put one on her vision board. She kept the dream of her son receiving his new kidney before her eyes consistently. And guess what after 10 years of waiting, but only four months of keeping the dream consistently before her eyes, Andre received his brand new kidney.

Celia W. – Florida

Displaying Your Vision - A Vision for Greater Influence through TV Appearances, Larger Venues

I'm so excited about what God is doing in and through your life and ministry and I want you to know how my life was forever impacted, transformed and changed.

I heard you speak one time, in Dallas, Texas. I drove 4 hours after the meeting to come back to my home near Houston, Texas. I was so impacted and inspired about having a dream board because you said that our lives follow after what we look at every day. I had a dream of living debt-free. I had a dream of being invited to be a guest on certain television show. I had a dream of raising up millions of soul winners to win billions of souls across the earth.

I had two small bedrooms in my home and I took a pencil and a string and drew an arch on the wall that night after I left your meeting. I went out of town to minister the gospel at a great church and a contractor knocked out this wall and we turned these rooms into an incredible dream suite. I don't only have a dream board, I put together a dream wall! I posted everything I'm believing for right here on my dream wall. I wrote it down on index cards, I posted it on my dream wall. I posted pictures, visuals of raising up multitude of soul winners and all the different things I was trusting God for.

Well, I want you to know, once I knocked the wall out and got my dream wall up, I came out of debt. The only thing I owe is on my home and I'm believing God to pay that off. I began to be invited to speak at some of the greatest churches in America and the world that is on my dream wall. I began to be invited to be a guest on these great television shows, where I have the opportunity and the platform to share with the world how Jesus Christ loves us and how He saves.

Terri, you are my super hero. I am one of your biggest cheerleaders. I am one of your biggest fans, because your message changed and transformed my life forever.

Debra G. – Texas

Once the Board Is Up - A Vision to See Greeting Cards in Gift Shops

Terri,

Thank you so much for being such an inspiration to me. I started watching your podcast back in 2010 and it was such a big help. When you told about the importance of having a vision and putting it on paper, it was a big eye opener for me. Then when you talked about your dream board in your office, I got so excited and created one as well. I put on that dream board my biggest desires and one of them was to have my illustrations published by Papyrus greeting cards. I wanted to see my work with gold glitter in a fancy Papyrus packaging. Every time I would go in a bookstore, in the greeting cards section, I would go to the Papyrus section and dream. I would tell God that I will be there too! The day came when I received an email from Papyrus inviting me to collaborate with them. I was so excited! Then months later, my card was made, exactly how I wanted. Now it is sold in Papyrus stores. I hope that this story inspires many to go for it, to dream even when you have no idea how it's going to come to pass. All you need is a dream and believe that God will do it. It's a matter of time, it was on my dream board for about 3 years but the result is so worth waiting for!

Daria

The Law of Attraction at Work - A Vision for a Baby

I have had the privilege of hearing you speak at several conferences and I know you are always saying to keep your dreams in front of you, so I had to share my story with you! In January 2013 my husband and I had a miscarriage around 9 weeks. We continued trying, but just couldn't get pregnant again. We had even started talking about adoption and fertility doctors. But I knew God would give us a baby in His time. Around August of 2014 we bought crayola bathtub crayons and wrote all over our shower walls, scriptures, positive confessions, business goals, in one corner I wrote "Baby in 2015" and right next to it was Thessalonians 5:16-18. I would speak it every morning in the shower! For Christmas my husband and I even bought each other little baby clothes and shoes because we knew our baby would be coming. In January, exactly two years and one day after our first baby (who we named Hope) went to heaven, we found out we were expecting again! After the first ultrasound when they measured the baby to determine exact age, I counted backwards and discovered that we conceived this baby on January 1st! God literally gave us our baby in 2015 on the first day of January!

Bethany W. – Virginia

Who Should See Your Dreams? - A Vision for a Husband, a House, and a Business

I've always understood the scripture in Habakkuk that says write the vision, make it plain so those who read it can run with it. But I never related it to being able to see it. I related it more being able to write it. I know I was believing God for my husband and I had been single for over 20 years and about 6 months before I met my husband I decided to really get seri-

*ous about writing a petition. I wrote down everything I was
believing God for so my eyes could see it.*

*And I would just confess every single day what I was
believing for and I could see it. The more I saw it the more
I believed it. And actually, when I met my husband, 90 days
after I met him we were married because I knew when I saw
him it's what I had been seeing all along by the scriptures I
had been writing down.*

*In 2012 I learned about vision boards and got together
with a group of women to create vision boards. After 2 hours
of working on it, my board was still mostly blank. I realized I
didn't really have a clear vision for what I was believing God
for. I knew God wanted to do big things, I wanted him to do
big things, but I really couldn't see it in my mind's eye.*

And so I read Terri's book, Imagine Big *and it was life
changing. She talked about just closing your eyes and learning to dream. We started the year with a new vision board.*

*My husband and I had spent nearly every weekend dili-
gently looking for a new home and new office building for our
marketplace ministry. For a year we looked every weekend.*

*Four months after I completed the vision board I saw a
home one night on the internet that we had not seen before.
We really don't know how we could have missed it. But I think
it's because I would never have dreamed of looking at that
home in the first place. I wouldn't have dreamed that big! But
I cut a picture out and put it on the vision board. I remember
the night that my husband and I looked at the home and we
were on the second floor. There was a balcony that overlooked
the property and I thought I was in Hawaii! The beauty of it,
the location. I was overwhelmed at the extravagance and the
pool, the waterfall, the palm trees. And then reality just hit
me. I looked at my husband and I said, "Honey, what are we
doing? Why are we looking at a home this extravagant? It's*

more than we need." And my husband looked at me, I'll never forget in a million years what he said. He said, "Honey, if you don't want to receive all God's goodness that He has for us I'm sure He can find somebody else He wants to give this home to." Those words pierced my heart and I realized I had been discounting for many years the great things God wanted to do in my life.

Two weeks after that conversation on the balcony, and four months after completing my vision board, my husband and I were signing a contract not only on our new home but on an office building for our marketplace ministry too.

Here's the part that is so great, so much greater than anything I could have ever dreamed or imagined. Two days before my husband and I were going to sign the contract, we both heard in our spirit that we were to owe no man anything but to love Him and the Lord wanted us to pay cash for both properties. It seemed virtually impossible. In order to do that we had to pretty much deplete an entire lifetime of investments in order to pay cash for the home. We had a big need, we were needing our finances to be restored. So we took that largest seed we had left and we planted it into a ministry and we believed God that before the year was over He would restore our financial situation and our accounts back to the way it was.

In January, I started my vision board.

In May, God delivered a brand new home and office buildings.

In December of that same year, God not only restored our accounts but they were even greater than before we started.

I am so grateful to Terri Savelle Foy Ministries for giving me the resources and the tools to be able to have clear vision and courage to dream big. Thank you so much!

Diana S. – Texas

What to Do While You're Waiting – A Vision for a Mission Trip and a Business

Some friends from my church attended a conference where Terri Savelle was speaking in Tyler, Texas. I wasn't able to go, but they brought back some good materials, including a copy of "My Personal Dreams and Goals" workbook.

I began to write the vision and make it plain according to Habakkuk 2. To my surprise, God began to make these dreams and goals happen. One of them was that I wanted to be apart of a mission group. My husband was going to India on a ministry trip, there was a cancellation, and they needed another speaker to fill in. I was able to go and be one of the speakers. At that time I was a Sunday school teacher to about 15 people. I would say "I'm not believing the handful but I'm believing for the hundreds." I got to India and I had an opportunity to speak to about 27,000 people! Because I wrote it down and I made it clear, God did even greater than I asked. I was not just part of the team, but I was actually a speaker.

I also wrote down that I wanted to own my own business. I had been a daycare director at my church for many years. There was man in town selling a daycare center and he offered to us for a very large amount. We weren't able to do it so we said we would just wait and pray about it. Well a few months later he approached us and said he needed to get rid of this business and that he believed he should sell it for $1. So he gave us this business for $1, this fully operating preschool. God has blessed it, it's full and it's a business opportunity that I wasn't expecting, but God made a way by writing it down.

So writing down things in our dream book or making a dream board really works. I'd encourage anybody that's stuck in a place where they feel like God is not doing the things you are believing for—I would encourage you to write it down in a dream book.

The dream book has made a difference in my life. Since 2012 our goals have happened, from a house, car, 2 new businesses—God has really given us the desires of our hearts because we have believed the word Habakkuk 2 write the vision make it plain on paper and he that sees it will run with it. So I encourage you today to make sure you begin to write your dreams and see if God won't take it and take it even further than your wildest imagination. God is faithful and His word is true. So just believe it, write it down, and just as Terri as given us the message, believe and you will see God take care of all of it.

Tammy H. – Texas

The Hidden Key - A Vision for a Significant Seed

During our engagement last fall, my fiance received an IRS bill for $2,700. Finances were very tight for both of us since we elected not to live together until our wedding, which meant double bills until then. Thankfully, we already made a conscience decision to have the Word at the center of our decisions, not money and tithed on every income coming into our homes. As far as our bank accounts were concerned the IRS bill could have been $27 million – it was well out of our natural means. My fiance submitted the paperwork required to prove the reported error and thought the matter closed. Shortly after returning from our honeymoon we received another IRS notification that we are still liable for the full $2,700. I sowed a significant seed of $200 (our entire monthly food budget), declaring that God would continue to provide. We cast the care of the matter onto our Lord Jesus and I am shouting for joy over the last IRS letter! CASE CLOSED. Not *only that but we now have money in our savings, a pantry full of food, and plenty left over to give to others! We serve a faithful God! Thank you for teaching us how to stay strong and the value of sowing significant seed!*

Courtney S. – South Dakota

APPENDIX A
HOST A VISION BOARD GROUP OR PARTY

Hosting a vision board small group or a one-night party can bring such fulfillment to your life. You, as the host, will be pivotal in helping others dismiss a life of stagnation and become energized to go after their dreams.

Begin by inviting some friends to embark on a life-changing journey of achieving their dreams. Depending on the duration of your vision board parties, whether it is a multiple-week small group gathering or a one-time party you plan to host, I have provided a format for both types of vision board gatherings to help you. Implement the format that works best for you and your desire for hosting these inspiring meetings.

Remember, vision boards are a starting point of dream achievement. They are not the end-all "magic" board that makes fairy-tale living possible. Vision board parties are useless and ineffective if they are simply turned into a "scrap-booking on a bulletin board" event. That's why I encourage follow-up gatherings more than just a one-time event, especially for people starting to learn about developing and pursuing their dreams and goals. The weekly group setting will allow you to encourage and influence each other to implement successful routines and behaviors that can bring about the desired results.

One of the greatest benefits of throwing a vision board party is the accountability it provides. Making a vision board sounds great and most people get inspired to locate their scissors and pick up a poster board; however, when it comes down to actually making the board, it can seem like a lot of work too. Getting together with others will crush procrastination and inspire you and your friends to take action.

Remember, a vision board is as unique as the individual designing it. It is simply a collection of pictures and words that describe each person's ideal future. Although I have expressed my personal style of listing my top ten goals for the year, as well as bigger aspirations that may occur over the next several years, there is not really a right or wrong way to design your board. Yours and your participant's boards might communicate their dreams for this year or for this decade. Choose what works best for each individual to keep them motivated on their fulfillment.

Just to reiterate why I choose to display my immediate annual goals is simply for the purpose of staying encouraged by their fulfillment as opposed to only displaying huge dreams that may require a ten-year span to acquire. It can be very demotivating to look at the same board for ten or twelve years and still see nothing achieved. I also like to have a personal vision board and a separate vision board for my ministry.

I've created a series of videos about the purpose of vision boards and how to use them effectively. Go to www.terri.com for access and to share them with your group to inspire them and start the countdown to your event.

Tips for Hosting Your Own Vision Board Small Group

Invite 6-12 people. Smaller groups like this help to create a comfortable environment for conversations, the ability to communicate dreams and goals, as well as give and receive encouragement.

Let them know about the vision board kits available from us at www.terri.com before you meet. This kit includes: *Dream It. Pin It. Live It.* book, *Dream It. Pin It. Live It.* workbook, one cork board, decorative push pins, some of my favorite motivational phrases, confessions, and Bible verses, all in a convenient carrying box. The book and workbook will serve as the learning map for your group.

Week 1: Welcome and discussion on chapters 1 and 2.

Chapter 1: Give Yourself Permission to Dream

Chapter 2: The Power of the Pen

Assignment: Start the "101 Dreams" list. Encourage your group to write as many as they can without the pressure of finishing the list.

Week 2: Discuss writing "101 Dreams" assignment and chapters 3 and 4.

Chapter 3: Your Top Ten Goals

Chapter 4: Design Your Board

Assignment: List your top ten goals for the next 12-18 months. Bring supplies for vision board party at the next gathering.

Week 3: Vision Board Party

Have fun decorating and designing your boards together.

Week 4: Discuss chapters 5 and 6.

Chapter 5: Display Your Destiny

Chapter 6: Once the Board is Up

Week 5: Discuss chapters 7 and 8.

Chapter 7: The Law of Attraction in Action

Chapter 8: Don't Share Big Dreams with Small Minds

Week 6: Discuss chapters 9 and 10 and prayer

Chapter 9: What to Do While You're Waiting

Chapter 10: The Hidden Key to Living Your Dreams

Pray over each person's dreams and goals.

Tips for Hosting a One-Night Vision Board Party

#1. Invite 6-12 people. Keep the guest list minimal in order to have room for guests to work on their vision boards. Larger groups can make it harder for those attending to share their dreams and goals. Encourage your guests to think about their dreams prior to the party.

#2. Let your group know about the vision board kits available from us at www.terri.com. If you are not planning to use our vision board kit, then encourage the participants to bring their own vision board to the party which could include a poster board, cork board or a magnetic board.

#3. Ask the participants to bring a collection of magazines, postcards, or brochures that they don't mind sharing and cutting into pieces. The more variety, the better.

#4. Personal photos. Using personal images on the board enables you to clearly see yourself living that dream. Ask guests to bring a variety of their own photographs to pin next to their goals.

#5. Additional items to request or provide: Glue, glitter, stickers, stamps, markers, motivational phrases, scrap-booking supplies (this can range from a broad variety of visuals such as "destination stickers" for those wanting to take a dream trip to miniature graduation caps symbolizing your dream of obtaining a college degree, etc).

#6. Every gathering is better with food! Whether you provide snacks, prepare a meal, or have everyone bring something to share, having something available to eat will help make your time together even better.

Have fun together. Inspire each other to travel to new places, explore new territories, learn a new language or skill, enroll in a class, and to dream big!

Encourage guests to not leave until at least three items are on their board. Many people will have great intentions and truly want to finish their board once they get home, but the reality is, months will pass by with the board unfinished and dreams still unrealized. They can always add to it, but having at least three top goals to pursue is a great place to start.

Remind your participants that their vision board is a visual reminder of where they intend to be. This activity is for the purpose of identifying their true dreams and clari-fying their immediate goals. This is a powerful tool to help your goals become more tangible and focused. This visual imagery enables you to see yourself living the dreams, plans, and purposes God's given you.

APPENDIX B
VISION BOARD SAMPLES
A Variety of Dreams Displayed

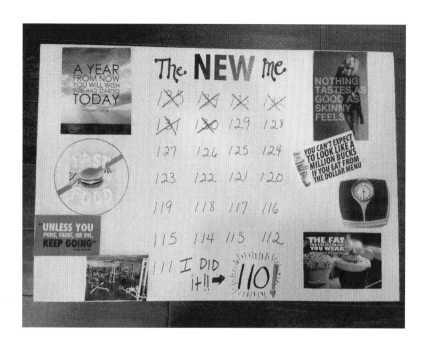

NOTES

1. http://www.doseofbliss.com/celebrities-whose-vision-boards-came-true/

2. ibid

3.http://www.usc.edu/dept/pubrel/specialevents/commencement/documents/PastSpeeches-Schwarzenegger

4. http://www.bulletproofmusician.com/what-happens-when-arnold-schwarzenegger-puts-his-mind-on-something/

5. http://www.steveharveytv.com/act-like-a-success-taking-the-lid-off-the-jar/

6. http://webcache.googleusercontent.com/search?q=cache:WEMGO-z6PjkEJ:www.evancarmichael.com/Entrepreneur-Advice/448/summary.php+&cd=5&hl=en&ct=clnk&gl=us

7. Martin, Dave, *The 12 Traits of the Greats: The Twelve Undeniable Qualities of Uncommon Achievers, and How You Can Master Them In Your Life... RIGHT NOW!*, Tulsa, OK: Harrison House, 20111, p.27.

8. Osteen, Joel, *Daily Readings From Your Best Life Now: 90 Devotions For Living At Your Full Potential* Nashville, TN: Warner Faith, 2005

9. http://www.victorycoaches.com/2014/11/12/early-success-goals-famous-arnold-schwarzenegger-plus-video/

10. https://www.youtube.com/watch?v=aE5-iFKBMIo

11. http://www.oprah.com/oprahs-lifeclass/What-Oprah-Learned-from-Jim-Carrey-Video

12. https://www.youtube.com/watch?v=kKvcNYzkip4

13. Morgan, John Rowley, *Climb Your Ladder of Success Without Running Out of Gas!: The Simple Truth on How to Revitalize Your Body and Ignite Your Energy for Lifelong Success*, James Publishing (December 1, 2007)

14. https://www.youtube.com/watch?v=8rRnTgkQ_1s

15. *Great at Any Age - Who Did What From Age 1 to 100... and Beyond*, Hallmark, 2009

16. http://www.oprah.com/oprahs-lifeclass/What-Oprah-Learned-from-Jim-Carrey-Video

17. http://www.doseofbliss.com/celebrities-whose-vision-boards-came-true/

18. Nicholson, Scott. *Seeds of Atonement*,

19. http://michaelhyatt.com/5-reasons-why-you-should-commit-your-goals-to-writing.html

20. Klaussen, Henriette Anne, *Write It Down, Make It Happen: Knowing What You Want And Getting It*, Fireside Books; 1st edition (January 3, 2001)

21. Orman, Suze. *The 9 Steps to Financial Freedom*, p. 31.

22. http://www.huffingtonpost.com/fred-whelan-and-gladys-stone/lou-holtzs-compelling-que_b_794675.html

23. Osteen, Joel. *Readings from Become a Better You*, p. 60.

24. Staples, Walter Doyle. *Think Like a Winner*, p. 174

25. Hill, Napoleon, *Think and Grow Rich Delux*, p. 141

26. https://www.youtube.com/watch?v=rtmHlLHdWRE

27. Rohn, Jim. *7 Strategies for Wealth and Happiness*,

28. www.BrianTracy.com/freegifts/goalsreportup.pdf

29. https://www.youtube.com/watch?v=rtmHlLHdWRE

30. www.blog.timesunion.com/careers/got-goals/1122/

31. https://www.youtube.com/watch?v=rtmHlLHdWRE

32. http://www.contentorial.com/5-new-years-resolutions-to-help-you-become-a-successful-content-writer-in-2013/

33. http://www.selfgrowth.com/articles/How_to_Use_a_Vision_Board_to_Activate_the_Law_of_Attraction.html

34. ibid

35. www.waldorfastoria3.hilton.com/en/about/history/index.html

36. www.waldorfnewyork.com/about-the-waldorf/hotel-history.html

37. Osteen, Dodie. *Healed of Cancer*

38. Jack Canfield and Mark Victor Hansen, *The Aladdin Factor*, Berkley, 1995, p. 76.

39. https://www.psychologytoday.com/blog/flourish/200912/seeing-is-believing-the-power-visualization

40. http://www.wholescience.net/2012/07/mental-rehearsal-key-to-improving-sports-performance/

41. http://www.oprah.com/oprahs-lifeclass/What-Oprah-Learned-from-Jim-Carrey-Video

42. http://www.bet.com/news/music/2013/12/05/tupac-shakur-predicts-death-in-unaired-interview.html

43. http://theboombox.com/dolla-rapper-who-correctly-predicted-their-own-death/

44. https://books.google.com/books?id=JQg3ETVSSNoC&pg=PT58&lpg=PT58&dq=Joseph+Grant+mental+suicide&source=bl&ots=-Ho6048S-N&sig=4Y7qE4PwT-FqcYyRL8koR70Rbu4&hl=en&sa=X&ved=0CFYQ6AEwCGoVChMI5bu5ubmLxwIVT5iICh1ApwA6#v=onepage&q=Joseph%20Grant%20mental%20suicide&f=false

45. www.miniature-earth.com

46. http://www.edisonfordwinterestates.org/

47. http://financebuzz.io/investing-millionaires-warren-buffett-stocks

48. https://www.youtube.com/watch?v=HHmK6GRasNI

49. Ziglar, Zig, "See You At The Top: 25th Anniversary Edition" audio series, New York: Simon & Schuster Audio/Nightingale-Conant; Abridged edition (June 16, 2009).

50. http://www.nydailynews.com/life-style/average-american-watches-5-hours-tv-day-article-1.1711954

51. http://www.marketingcharts.com/online/social-networking-eats-up-3-hours-per-day-for-the-average-american-user-26049/

52. http://www.entrepreneur.com/article/230918

53. https://books.google.com/books?id=tHv2_3Ob-jZ0C&pg=PT424&lpg=PT424&dq=average+person+commute+equivalent+of+college+education&source=bl&ots=lLez90Au-R&sig=OKIz9Oz20JkFc8l5JWpY2sX-3owo&hl=en&sa=X&ved=0CC4Q6AEwAmoVChMI5uD9kcqNxwIVR-RaUCh3TLwBt#v=onepage&q=average%20person%20commute%20equivalent%20of%20college%20education&f=false

54. https://www.youtube.com/watch?v=8rRnTgkQ_1s

55. https://books.google.com/books?id=XFg8BAAAQBAJ&printsec=-frontcover&dq=best+practices+in+literacy&hl=en&sa=X&ved=0C-B4Q6AEwAGoVChMIlKq-3vmOxwIViaOICh0LugMA#v=onepage&q=never%20read&f=false

56. https://www.jackcanfield.com/images/stories/JackCanfields-ReadingList-1.pdf

57. http://news.investors.com/management-leaders-and-success/013101-347206-basketball-player-larry-bird-grit-and-discipline-helped-him-lead-championship-teams.htm

58. https://www.youtube.com/watch?v=8rRnTgkQ_1s

59. https://www.youtube.com/results?search_query=will+smith+shares+his+secrets+of+success

60. https://www.youtube.com/watch?v=8rRnTgkQ_1s

61. Ramsey, Dave, *The Total Money Makeover A Proven Plan For Financial Fitness*, Nashville, TN: Thomas Nelson, 2009, p. 120.

62. https://www.youtube.com/watch?v=8rRnTgkQ_1s

63. https://www.youtube.com/watch?v=8rRnTgkQ_1s

64. https://www.youtube.com/watch?v=8rRnTgkQ_1s

Printed in Great Britain
by Amazon